DECLASSIFIED

*Moving beyond the dead end
of race in South Africa*

Gerhard Maré

JACANA

First published by Jacana Media (Pty) Ltd in 2014

10 Orange Street
Sunnyside
Auckland Park 2092
South Africa
+2711 628 3200
www.jacana.co.za

ISBN 978-1-4314-2020-9

Cover design by Niek de Greef
Set in Sabon 10.2/13.87pt
Printed and bound by Creda Communications
Job no. 002244

See a complete list of Jacana titles at www.jacana.co.za

DECLASSIFIED

'I learned about the importance of simultaneously maintaining a healthy respect for complexity and a great capacity for outrage'
– *Kathryn Mills about her father, sociologist C. Wright Mills*[1]

These words, by Kathryn Mills, I apply to a person who shaped my thinking at various stages and gave me the courage and the encouragement to continue with what I was doing and the explorations I will continue to do:
Neville Alexander (1936–2012)

Contents

Acknowledgements

What is offered here is located within my own historical journey as an individual in South Africa – fragments of which I will refer to directly. I have grappled immediately and personally with an autobiography lived throughout apartheid South Africa, and then into a democratic republic since 1994. The book has been written in a context where my thinking has, of necessity, been structured by my location at the University of Natal – 'merged' into the new University of KwaZulu-Natal (UKZN), with its name deliberately chosen, but inadvertently acknowledging the colonial, bantustan, ethnic and racialised past of this section of south-eastern Africa. Here I taught, and in some instances co-taught, for several years a graduate course on 'Race thinking and thinking about race'. This book continues the many conversations around the topic I had with local students and those drawn to Durban through the Global Studies Programme (globally selected and globally diverse, rewarding beyond most other teaching initiatives I have been involved in), whom I wish to thank. I acknowledge the inspiration and ideas of valued colleagues and friends; with special mention of the occasional (too many to name, but thanks to all of you) as well as continuing members of the 'Reading Group' since 1986 – Christopher Ballantine and Grahame Hayes.

The content also owes its existence to support from Ahmed Bawa while he was at the University of Natal and then the UKZN (he is now Vice-Chancellor of the Durban University of Technology). His critical thinking about the issue of race, long before and subsequently during the establishment of the Centre for Critical Research on Race and Identity, helped focus my ideas and inspire me to continue. The Centre (CCRRI), of which I was director from 2006 until 2012, provided a platform from which to initiate and support research, also on the issue addressed here, with a valued staff (Amanda Kinners, Orli Bass, Niall McNulty, Naretha

Pretorius, Yvonne Erasmus, Prinisha Badassy and Kira Erwin). The process of writing is indebted, in addition, to the intellectual stimulus of events such as the conferences on the Burden of Race, at the University of the Witwatersrand, and on Genetics and Race organised by Wilmot James; the symposium on Classification in 2011 at the CCRRI; the workshop 'Revisiting apartheid race categories', held at the University of the Witwatersrand; and the research and discussions initiated by the Ahmed Kathrada Foundation (AKF), the Human Sciences Research Council (HSRC), the Gauteng City-Region Observatory (GCRO), and the Public Affairs Research Institute (PARI).

Completing the book would certainly not have been possible without the privilege and pleasure of fellowships at the Stellenbosch Institute for Advanced Study (STIAS) during 2012 and again in 2013. It provided the ideal space for reflection and interaction, and concentrated writing. My heartfelt appreciation to its director and staff, and those who were fellows during my stays. The National Research Foundation in South Africa (NRF) provided financial support for the writing and editing of the book, for which I am grateful.

Karen Press edited and provided references, information, questions and discussion, which were extremely valuable and essential to the completion of the book. Further editing involvement came from Russell Martin and Kira Erwin. Academic readers provided challenging comments. Dan Maré was the first reader of the manuscript, and his responses were intellectually and motivationally important in the concluding phases of writing. Glenn Moss has been an essential contributor to my ideas since the early 1970s and has certainly kept me on my toes. I take responsibility for what appears in the book.

My sons, Dan and Jo, born in the decade before the transition, have now spent most of their lives living in a democratic society. They have been in the background to my thoughts while puzzling over these issues, as they were in 1993 when I dedicated a previous book, on ethnicity and its dangerous misuse in political mobilisation, to them – they are having to live and act in the world we have created. Thembisa Waetjen has been with me throughout most of my life in post-1994 South Africa. Thank you, T, for so much.

Introduction

I was as convinced then as I am now of the book's central claim
– that race is easy to think but difficult to think about, that it is
experienced as a self-evidently natural part of the modern world,
and that it is contrived in the extreme but in ways that people
hardly notice.

– Lawrence Hirschfeld[1]

The metonymic image of banal nationalism is not a flag which is
being consciously waved with fervent passion; it is the flag hanging
unnoticed on the public building.

– Michael Billig[2]

The world in the second decade of the twenty-first century is an insecure
space for most of its human and non-human inhabitants. Maybe it has
always been so, but never before have our various fates been so intertwined,
so infected, inflected and affected by what happens elsewhere. Nor till
now have humans held their global political and environmental future in
their collective hands, with so little sign of taking shared responsibility.

The global context and its consequences for material conditions
in South Africa, the primary focus of my writing, have had profound
negative and constricting effects in the economic sphere. Capitalism is
surviving today more clearly through crises (especially for the poorer
majority of populations). The costs experienced by billions, and the
absurd and often criminal benefits of that survival that accrue to a tiny
minority, too, are felt across the globe, unequally. Capitalism's survival
is taking place on the basis of close protection and facilitation from the
state or groupings of states. In this way, economic disasters are boosting

the existence of the nation-state despite (or maybe even because of) trends towards global integration. Global integration probably thrusts us all into crises rather than into the wishful benefits of global citizenship some argued for; into the borderless terrain where decisions made are based on the gluttony of locally operating capital rather than taking into account globally human, moral or future-thinking concerns; into the political space where claims for nationhood and other unchanging identities take root – against widely held expectations of a less locally defined and more flexible world of a mere thirty years ago, with its occasional imaginings of cosmopolitanism.

At the same time, these shared problems are stimulating searches for alternative ways of ordering the arenas of production and consumption, of distribution and redistribution, of existing within shared social spaces. We are inevitably social animals. The search for creativity, for imagination, for co-habitation, for collective solutions continues, but under harsh conditions, unfavourable to such endeavours. In many cases they threaten established interests. Those are the interests that thrive on disorganisation, on fear, on blame of anyone but themselves and their doings.

The first decade of this new century has passed, and this book, started several years ago, is only now completed, written so many times over the years. It is now committed to being shared, but never to be completed with confident final statements on unambiguous solutions. What is this attempt aimed at? I wish to capture, in an argument (shared with others) and with a tiny fraction of the illustrative evidence available to me, the insidious and invidious ways in which notions of race remain the unquestioned bedrock of our thinking – here in South Africa and in many other parts of the world. Difference (rather than diversity), as a way of life and in various forms, continues, as there is little reward for reflection on what we share in common as a society, rather than on notions of what divides us. The latter reflect a specific and largely exclusive way of seeing the world – in South Africa their vicious consequences are illustrated above all by violence against women and children, against some of those who do not share our nationality or culture, those who are perceived to be different in their sexuality. Tentatively, I suggest alternatives through asking for debate, by implication through the argument I make, and with some concrete suggestions. Mostly, I hope to do so by simply gaining recognition that there is a question to be asked.

Can I suggest ways in which we not only need to but could go beyond the racialised world we inhabit? I have taken the liberty of using the personal at times to make it clear why I have engaged in this contested field of exploration. The first 44 years of my life occurred under white-ruled South Africa, which brought actual and potential benefits not available to most fellow South Africans, and the obligation, shared with many (but taken up by a minority among the racialised beneficiaries), to struggle against that system and its skewed privileges.

A slightly fuller narrative of my life than the descriptive points of race allocation, sex and age would begin with a brief introduction to growing up in, and being socialised into, Afrikanerdom, a fractious ethnic fraction of the 'white' race category. I was born in 1946 in Estcourt in Natal, then a province of the Union of South Africa. My father was a junior civil servant there at the time. Later, he was to serve as Bantu (previously Native and later Black) Affairs Commissioner posted to various villages and towns in or on the edge of what became the KwaZulu bantustan. He was well qualified for these postings through his fluency in the Zulu language, and his familiarity with and respect for what was, and is, perceived as 'traditional' Zulu society, customs and values. Here, the 2006 novel by Shaun Johnson, *The Native Commissioner*, carried many familiar memories for me, despite the (at times) different political and ideological positions held by the two civil servants.[3]

My mother, a teacher for most of her working life, was raised in a loyal National Party farming family in the north-east of the Orange Free State, closest to the village of Kestell and the town of Harrismith, a woman who had studied at the University of the Orange Free State in Afrikaans (she graduated in the early 1940s), and yet had her first teaching job at the English-language St Mary's school in Natal. My maternal grandfather (born in 1894) fled with his mother and avoided capture by the British army during the South African War (or so the story holds). As a founding member of the National Party (NP) in 1914, he remained loyal until his death in 1949. He was one of the 25 party members from the Orange Free State who walked out of a 1934 meeting to discuss *samesmelting* (fusion) between the South African Party (SAP) and the NP (from which the United Party emerged).[4] These dissidents gathered at the Oranje-koffiehuis (a coffee shop) to continue the NP. Language was of the essence in organising and mobilising Afrikaners and NP members. I found a letterhead that my mother used while a student that well captures the form such mobilisation took. There were two main injunctions: *Praat, lees en skryf Afrikaans* (Speak, read and write Afrikaans) and *Moenie vergeet om 'n Afrikaner te wees nie* (Do not forget to be an Afrikaner). Language, as cultural signifier, was to play a very important part in my life. 'Importance' in a narrative such as this is, of course, a matter of hindsight, but it should become clear why I make such a claim.

Secondly, mention of a scrapbook I prepared for *Republiekdag* (Republic Day), the first one in 1961, would help illustrate those formative events and participations in my life – I also kept one on the launch of *Sputnik 1* and subsequent space exploration. The political consciousness, rather than everyday racialised social common sense, within which I was raised was that of language (Afrikaans) and its obvious synonymy with being (white) *Afrikaner* (against *die Engelse* (also white)) and its importance in *die Republiekeinse strewe* (the striving for a republic). For me, at least initially, this dimension of politics, rather than *rassepolitiek* (race politics), dominated in political memory, though obviously not in lived life, for even here the contradictions of existence in South Africa were unavoidably present. Being *Afrikaner* was, in its mobilisation but not in its individual lived reality, based on language (synonymous with culture). Politics (usually contained within the dominant National Party and its core policies, including apartheid); religion (and here the Nederduits Gereformeerde Kerk (Dutch Reformed Church) predominated); and always whiteness, as race – although this fault-line had the *kleurlingvraagstuk* (the Coloured question), as it was referred to, hovering as a moral reminder of the bizarreness of race classification and exclusion.

The farm on which I spent my early childhood was not a successful venture. I lived an adventurous boyhood there during my pre-teen years, with no comparison to hand. My father was trying to become a farmer rather than being one, a role he had opportunistically and ambitiously taken on after my mother inherited the property on my grandfather's death. Maybe he thought that farming ran in the blood of all Afrikaners. As we were too far away from any school (for those classified as whites), and there was too little money to send the children to boarding school, my mother taught us. This service was extended to children from neighbouring farms, but, if I remember correctly, there were never more than five of us in the front room of our corrugated iron house. It was all in Afrikaans, properly so as English was seen as the language of the oppressor, and the province was dominated by Afrikaans-speaking white people. English-speaking South Africans were regarded, when perceived as a category, as members of the United Party and local representatives of the British Empire, which had employed both concentration camps and scorched earth policies during what is now known as the South African War, a war in which the Orange Free State bore the brunt. This bitter struggle was also variously called the *Tweede Vryheidsoorlog* (Second War of Liberation), Anglo-Boer War or simply *die Boere-oorlog.*

Speaking English in shops when going on holiday in the 1950s to the Natal coast, where winters were so mild that it was a major treat for us *Vrystaters* (Free Staters), was a point of tension for my mother. She often insisted on being served in Afrikaans. There was a fear that Afrikaans would be swamped by English, based also on experiences of anglicisation immediately after the defeat of the Boer republics. The language struggle at what became the University of the Orange Free State was, in the 1920s, already founded on whether the institution should be bilingual or Afrikaans only.[5] Hannes Haasbroek notes that, especially in the 1940s, the National Party was much more than a political party. It was, rather, a *kultuurverskynsel* (a cultural phenomenon), a 'movement' representing the language, educational, religious and political aspirations of a *volk* (people).[6] Unlike my mother, my father had completed his schooling at an English-language school, Glenwood High, still today one of the top public schools in the English-speaking part of the city of Durban.

All these statements on politics and language relate to a 'white' social world. My early experiences were encompassed within that world, with exceptions, some of which I will mention below. New locations and events increasingly contextualised my own life within the wider reality of the country and further dimensions of its race and class struggles. A photograph which I had forgotten about until paging through my mother's photo albums after her death, along with the event which it captured in 1963, reflects my total immersion in that distinctive racialised world and some of its ways of being; a moment in a predictable timeline: Gerhard Maré, cadet of the year, shown participating in a totally light-skinned world, in a ceremony demanded only of light-skinned boys who carried the appropriate identity document, with the obligation to defend the existing order against all-comers.

Thirdly, reference should be made in this personal journey, despite the first two points, to an openness to words and ideas through a book culture in our family, even during my early childhood. And through exposure in schooling to the less expected route: from the farm school, where I was taught in Afrikaans by my mother; to a very small English-only junior school in southern Natal (where a teacher, for some reason, gave me a copy of a book on the Russian Revolution to read – it could even have been Trotsky's history); to a dual-medium (English and Afrikaans) high school in Newcastle in conservative northern Natal; and subsequently to the Durban campus of the somewhat liberal and overwhelmingly segregated University of Natal. The last-mentioned move was probably the most important, as it reflected a deliberate choice against what was expected of an Afrikaner boy, but one that was not resisted by my parents. It was a choice that had no political motivation that I can claim. Rebellion was not how I experienced taking that option. Previous relocations had taken place because of my father's transfers to different magisterial districts. Here, at the University of Natal, it was my decision to study engineering in Durban – with my parents' support – probably because English-speaking friends from Newcastle were heading there.

There are narratives that could try to capture what I gained from each of the educational locations, but that is for more casual reflection than the focus I attempt here. More revealing of the English–Afrikaans divide is an event that occurred when I did nine months of 'basic military training' as a conscript with other white boys and young men in the South African Defence Force in 1965, immediately upon leaving school and before heading to the University of Natal. My closest friends during this period were two English-speakers, an association that led directly to my being punched by an Afrikaner lad, coincidentally from the same part of the Free State where I had grown up. He resented my friendships across the language barrier. A note of some relevance to the odd picture of the time: despite increasing political tension, only a few years after the Sharpeville massacre, the banning of the African National Congress (ANC) and the decision by that movement to launch an armed struggle, our military instructors insisted on calling our 'enemy', against which we were being trained in still 'conventional warfare', the mysteriously named *Harry die Rus* (Harry the Russian). Maybe it was a labelling unique to this camp, maybe it stood for all things communist, but it remained with me through the years because of its bizarreness.

A fourth period – significant in retrospect, but merely experienced in the moment at the time – came in the late 1960s and 1970s, years which have since been called 'the Durban Moment', in reference to the legacy of Rick Turner and many others who were disturbing the taken-for-granted. Rick was, during the time of the 'Moment', a politics lecturer at the University of Natal, on the Durban campus, until he was banned by the apartheid state. This prevented him from teaching, publishing anything, and having his work read legally. Turner was assassinated in 1978 in his home in Durban, where I and several other young people had also lived at various stages. He died in the presence of his two young daughters, shot by a still unknown member of the apartheid security establishment. The 'Moment' refers to the coincidental congruence of people and their influences both then and subsequently, such as Steve Biko, the founder (with others) of the Black Consciousness Movement, and Rick Turner himself. Both were killed within a few months of each other. Steve Biko died of severe injuries sustained during a savage beating under interrogation by security police. That confluence was, however, marked by more than society-changing individuals – although the list of those who can be associated with that time and the ideas generated then, and whose influence continued to be felt during the 1980s and beyond, is noteworthy.[7] The period included a fresh stage of labour organisation and labour strikes of an unprecedented magnitude, cultural ferment and creativity, underground and open politics, large-scale Zulu ethnic mobilisation, and much more, all occurring in a historically tumultuous and fractious part of south-eastern Africa.

I had changed academic direction at the end of 1966, realising that engineering was not for me, and began a BA degree that ultimately resulted in my majoring in English, Afrikaans-Nederlands and Politics. It opened up contacts, reading, university courses and aspects of a lifestyle that reflected American and British versions of counter-cultural 'hippiedom', adapted to local conditions. The last-mentioned was important largely because it took very little deviation from the conservative norm of white South African society for individuals to be seen as a threat to social stability and political security. Music, dress, sexual morality, living spaces, drugs and the general politics of rebellion disturbed notions of the behaviour expected of the ideal white young person. The fact of deliberate classification as a racialised minority made any deviation even more threatening to the order imposed on all, black and white, and accepted by most whites. The rejection of military service for political or religious reasons, for example, drew strong reaction from the state.[8] While Rick Turner was neither a participant in nor a supporter of this 'hippie counter-culture' direction in social rebellion (especially not that aspect fuelled by marijuana),[9] he did have an effect indirectly here too through his influential style of enquiry and his own out-of-the-South-African-ordinary lifestyle. He proposed the need for disturbance, at every opportunity, of the taken-for-granted. He advocated the 'necessity of utopian thinking' and illustrated its application in his book *The Eye of the Needle* to escape the blinkers imposed by the apartheid state.[10] I will return to this mode of envisioning a future, to dislodge the common sense of the present.

The fifth period I could extract in this journey of discovery was one of 'active recovery' after a spell of detention in a prison in Pretoria during the Breyten Breytenbach case in 1975. This phase, which also led to a rewarding change of direction, started in late 1975.[11] My detention occurred during the second year of my serving as Social Action Officer in NUSAS, the National Union of South African Students. By now I was a totally different political being from the one who started his university career in 1966. When I was released from detention, my mother asked me, 'Where did we go wrong?' I could assure her that, from my own perspective, I would thank them for allowing me sufficient space and confronting me with sufficient ideas – even if unintentionally – to be able to respond to possibilities way beyond the obvious path then the lot of young Afrikaners. It was probably not the assurance she wanted, but she did not argue.

In late 1975, I accepted an invitation to take up a place in the newly introduced interdisciplinary Development Studies Programme at graduate level at the University of the Witwatersrand in Johannesburg. This was undertaken during the same year as the 1976 Soweto student uprising. Our class of three was also disrupted by the detention and appearance of one of its members, Glenn Moss, in what became known as the 'NUSAS trial'. Some of the courses demanded rigorous exposure to a wide and challenging range of ideas and theorists – especially Marxism and Marxists – which made this a formative period, where critical reflection, writing, and the deliberate and strategic dissemination of ideas came to dominate my life and subsequent activism and employment. It was, in some ways, far removed from the comparative literature honours degree I had completed in 1972, though both stimulated interdisciplinary approaches to social analysis.

Elements that relate fairly directly to my engagement with the central topic of this book had now been put in place and confirmed. My journey beyond the racialised boundaries imposed by apartheid had extended through participation in a student world that included people like Steve Biko and others too numerous to name here, and through breaking the class barrier in my involvements in the wider society. Being involved in worker organisation, and in thinking about and collecting information that deliberately set out to advance the interests of an exploited class, was a privilege that enabled me to engage with aspects of the variety of South African life. This sixth period, from 1976, can be characterised as one of investigation into the methods and content of political mobilisation, a world in which I had been raised and had experienced first-hand, albeit unreflectively, as an Afrikaner – religion, culture, politics, and a notion of historical origin and destiny. The mobilisations that interested me were those in reaction to, and also those hosted by, apartheid policies of race and of ethnicity.

In the background, always, was the question of why some see through the simplifications and purpose of such mobilisation, and reject the obvious advantages and apparent security, the strong sense of community, that go with it. What creates 'traitors', 'dissidents', those who have to be cast out of the fold (Beyers Naudé, Breyten Breytenbach and Bram Fischer, to name just three very public 'Afrikaner' figures), when they have not already chosen to exit themselves? I can find an event that indicates very early discomfort with the inescapable inclusion in Afrikanerdom, even if then little more than a raised eyebrow and an unarticulated resentment. My first year at the University of Natal in 1966 was also an election year for white South Africans.[12] Because I could not vote in the district where I was registered, I was entitled to a postal vote. An Afrikaans-speaking official brought this around, and as I handed the sealed envelope back to him he asked, '*Het jy reg gestem*?' (Did you vote correctly?) Of course, I knew immediately what he was implying, namely a vote for the National Party. Such a 'right' vote he was entitled to expect, because I was a fellow Afrikaner, from a largely Afrikaans-speaking part of the province of Natal. The episode was little more than a disturbance, probably because I saw myself as setting out on a new, more open phase of my life, but it has remained with me. There would be many others, illustrating in much more disturbing ways the contradictions and complexity of South African life.

These concerns about ethnic mobilisation and the fixing of such identity, of which the expected membership of *die volk* (the nation, people) was a reflection, were given firm direction when I took up employment at the University of Natal from 1984. Here, I taught, wrote and researched extensively on the mobilisation of ethnicity and its consequences, both in the region and nationally. It rang warning bells of familiarity with my own experience as an Afrikaner-raised fugitive from calls to ethnic solidarity and action. The form it took was Inkatha, a 'cultural liberation movement', and its content was Zuluness, from the mid-1970s to the transition in the early 1990s and beyond.[13] Zuluness is still the form its confirmation takes in the twenty-first century – for the tourist industry and again for political and economic mobilisation.

These concerns around identity and the deliberate description, mobilisation and maintenance of such social identities – and the reasons for such actions – are what inform this book, as they informed the establishment of the Centre for Critical Research on Race and Identity in 2006 at the University of KwaZulu-Natal, of which I was director till 2012. I should note that my own route as a white South African, born into the immediacy and omnipresent socialisation of Afrikaner apartheid, was very different from those of many with whom I came to associate most closely during my years as a student and in forms of activism. They were English-speaking and had had largely a liberal upbringing in terms of family and school. In contrast, I had to struggle *against* the consequences of my past – there was no familiar path and no family support during the years of questioning and escape. But I never expected that. I knew what my parents stood for and why those values had been such a certainty for them. School and religion had not prepared me in the slightest for the dramatic changes, either. On the contrary, my life had to be carved out against the consequences of my past in the new circles in which I found myself, now as the 'other' (in relation to English-speakers) that had (selectively) to become part of the 'us', a new group within which I moved socially and acted politically, and which was informed by values and ideas different from the overwhelming majority of our ascribed race group.

But I have also insisted on deliberately taking some of the aspects of the past with me, wilfully not denying their influence. For example, while most people know me as 'Gerry', a name given in junior school in the 1950s when fellow English-speaking pupils could not easily pronounce and maybe accept me as 'Gerhard', I have always published under the name Gerhard Maré. This reflects a refusal to be boxed into what is acceptable on occasions when I argue a case where it matters. Another aspect lay in my claiming as valuable the Afrikaans language and the literature created in it; and finding deep companionship with the many 'dissident Afrikaners' who left their mark in oppositional politics over the years, breaking the boundaries of social expectations and indicating the possibility of change, sometimes at great personal cost.

* * *

This book consists of three parts. The first chapter, which forms Part One, should be read as introductory. It concentrates on the general, the abstract, the scheme of analysis and presentation, and some of the concepts and language essential to that task, of which classification is central.[14] This is necessary because processes of categorisation and confirmation of already classified groups provide the strongest and essential thread that runs throughout the book. It is the process of 'sorting' that operates through society, creating templates for the silos of difference within which we live large parts of our lives. The central focus, obviously, is on the classification of human beings into 'races', a practice immediately demeaning of fellow human beings and bearing potentially horrifying consequences. Chapter 1 also locates these concepts within the historical social formation that is South Africa. A racialised and racist order of already existing groups was bequeathed to the apartheid politicians and theorists, and then gratefully built upon and adapted in various ways.

In Part Two, I discuss the regrettable continuity into a democratic ('post'-apartheid) South Africa of race thinking and race practices as well as racism. Why the unfortunate formal status of races in a society constitutionally committed to dignity, to non-sexism and non-racialism? I argue that the reason for the deliberate continuation of race classification, maintaining in many ways the silos of apartheid, is not sufficient and does not address the real concerns, which I believe should be the renewed starting point of debate. Furthermore, race classification carries inevitable seeds of conflict within itself.

Part Three is devoted to what it might mean to achieve a non-racial society. Both the necessity and the consequences of a process of rejecting the existence of races, as implied by non-racialism, are confronted here.

This final section could also have introduced the book, as it is in the notion of non-racialism that I believe the most hopeful possibility of a future beyond 'race' continues to lie. Non-racialism is not to be seen as colour-blindness – not in the least. Indeed, non-racialism relies on critical colour awareness.

This book is, therefore, about race thinking (also referred to as racialism), the way in which we accept 'race' as 'a self-evidently natural part of the modern world'. This is a world already classified whose validity 'we' accept – and I include my historical self and millions of fellow human beings in the nineteenth and twentieth centuries. But the book is also concerned with thinking *about* race, an issue 'difficult to think about', as Hirschfeld puts it in the epigraph to this Introduction. Reflecting on race is awkward, despite its being often met as a social reality. Maybe the difficulty lies in the common sense of everyday confrontation with our racialised selves and society. Confrontation becomes confirmation of what already is, unless our minds are opened to alternatives. The difficulty also resides in power relations that are inextricably linked to any allocation of social identity in fixed form: whether on the basis of gender, sexuality, race, religion or others. Power often enters and removes complexity from everyday life, or else thrives on the deliberate creation of complexity and contradiction to confuse rather than question.

I am motivated by the need to suggest and debate and research steps towards the promise such a world holds, 'beyond race', one in which we can live together imaginatively and open to the diversity each one of us presents, from within the starting point of our shared humanity. Some have already claimed a post-race world, but that is an absurdity and inflicts further indignity on those subject to racism in its many forms. Some have responded to such a goal by dismissing it as an exercise in futile utopian thinking. Perhaps, but it is no less necessary for that.

PART ONE

1

Thinking about race
and our racial legacy

Facts are linguistically meaningful entities which select out from
the stream of events what happened or what exists. But this means
that in order to be facts at all there must be a vocabulary in terms of
which they can be described. *Without a prior vocabulary which a
describer brings to a situation there would be no facts whatsoever.*
— Brian Fay[1]

In this chapter, I suggest ways in which we can employ available conceptual
tools, and create new ones, to explore a route of understanding that may
lead us to the seemingly impossible destination: a non-racial South Africa.
If we want to create a genuinely non-racial society, we cannot borrow,
unquestioningly, from the language of apartheid and the segregationist and
colonial eras the words that gave us races. In the search for alternatives,
we cannot accept the same practices, based on the vocabulary of 'what
we are', that the National Party deliberately used. Apartheid South Africa
was a social formation that did not provide the language to think past
itself, a society that deliberately suppressed such a language.

Indeed, the language of the dream of a non-racial country, of
motivation in struggles to realise this dream, had to be created under very
difficult circumstances. It needed — and needs — to be, simultaneously, a
language of possibility, of what could be, and one of questioning what
is; it could not and cannot restrict itself to description and confirmation
of the existing order, of 'things as they are now'. It is through a
questioning conversation — which implies curiosity about what others
in the conversation are saying, even if not necessarily acceptance of their
argument — that debate advances.

Neville Alexander, as conscious as he was of the power of language to affect people's material lives, and of the liberatory potential of language itself, had the following to say on this matter of the way words and labels close us off from alternatives, or lock us into a prior vocabulary, the one we have been given through the dominant ideas of our society:

> It is common cause in the social sciences today that social as well as individual identities are constructed, not 'given'. The state, or more generally, the ruling classes, in any society have the paradigmatic prerogative of setting the template on which social identities, including racial identities, are based. Subaltern groups and layers of such societies necessarily contest or accept these identities over time. In our own case, recent examples of such contestation are the categories of 'Bantu' and 'Coloured'. We must remember, however, that even though they are constructed, social identities seem to have a primordial validity for most individuals, precisely because they are not aware of the historical, social and political ways in which their identities have been constructed.[2]

The 'facts' of race belonging seem to have that 'primordial validity': they seem to have been there always; they serve our purposes in the present, because we have already learnt them, made them part of our way of describing and living the world around us.

If races, and the distinctions we use to identify different races, are socially constructed, not 'real' except in the way we think about them and in the actions that flow from that thinking, how do we speak about them when we want to challenge their existence? How do we distance ourselves from seeming to accept race as biologically real, and yet deal with its social reality? You may, for instance, follow the common practice of using quotation marks in your writings and also in conversation (with the help of raised hands and a delicate movement of your index fingers), to distance yourself from any possible implied meaning associated with the words you have nonetheless used, in this case to refer to these 'races' that do not exist. (The term 'so-called' fulfilled the same function as quotation marks in oppositional circles during the later years of the struggle against apartheid (and still does at times), especially when referring to 'Coloureds' as an apartheid race category.)

While I recognise the purpose of these and other distancing strategies, I also accept the need for non-erasure of racial terms. They remain analytically meaningful. This is so because of the continued use made of them to dominate and exploit, allocate life chances, and devalue the humanity of category members; but, most importantly, because of the claim that they remain essential in the project of creating a world in which they will have lost the dehumanising meaning we presently allocate to them. In one way, we have to keep them writ large, in order to evade the near-inevitable consequences of conflict they carry. In general, however, distancing strategies represent a (perhaps necessarily) formulaic challenge to the validity of race terminology. My argument in this book is that the issue has to be confronted and resolved in a more meaningful way than this uneasy 'quotation mark' approach.

Let me be clear at this early stage of my argument: I do not accept that there are biologically differentiated human social groups to be called races – biological groups, seen as 'natural', to which we can and should and do attach any generalisable and unchanging attributes of culture, physical ability, intelligence or whatever else. At the same time, I am not denying the commonsense continuation of the belief in races, with its actual or potential consequences for individuals and society as a whole, arising from actions informed by this belief. Nor do I deny the need to examine races as they featured in practice in the past and present and will regrettably continue to do. The prevalence of racism is but one obvious reason to attend to racialism.

When I use the term 'race' it will be to refer to the outcome of social processes undertaken and experienced by fellow humans in their efforts to give meaning to the world around them. The core of that meaning is an acceptance of the social world as consisting of identifiable groups, indisputable categories of people who are essentially locked into separate 'communities'. This process can refer not only to communities defined in terms of races, but also to other social communities that we create and accept (such as those of gender, sexuality, nationality, ethnicity). Robert Miles uses the term 'signification' for this labelling activity.[3] He argues that signification of the word 'race' comprises two selections. The first involves choosing 'biological or somatic characteristics [aspects relating to the body] in general as a means of classification and categorisation'. The second selection, according to Miles, involves choosing specific somatic characteristics 'as signifying a supposed difference between human beings'. In other words, we first decide (or have it decided for us) that the body carries race, and then we decide on a variety of specific and supposedly unique (to the group, not the individual) bodily characteristics, such as colour of skin, shape of facial features, hair texture and others, depending to a large extent on who we are and where we are when we learn to attach significance. It is necessary to add, as a third selection, or rather attribution, that of specific cultural traits or abilities or inabilities allocated to the races previously signified.[4]

When we signify, give meaning to, something, and that something is what we perceive to be distinguishable groups of races, I call that process 'racialisation', the process of socially constructing races. The philosopher Kwame Anthony Appiah has used the term 'racialism' to refer to sets of ideas about races that are the outcome of racialisation.[5] Racialism, according to Appiah, indicates an acceptance 'that there are heritable characteristics, possessed by members of our species, which allow us to divide them into small sets of races'. That they are 'heritable' means that if we are racialists, we know that no one can escape their 'race belonging' – we are born with our race – even if we have to learn this 'fact'. It is in the form of racialism that race thinking operates most extensively. In what follows, I will use the terms 'race thinking' and 'racialism' interchangeably to refer to a paradigm in which we accept that there are races, that we can tell what they are and who belongs to them, and that we can use such knowledge in our daily thinking and actions. In terms of this paradigm, if any individual among us rejects the notion of race, refuses to 'belong' to a race, someone else will have the power to insist that, whether you wish it or not, you are a member of a race. It is this paradigm that permeates post-1994 South Africa, as it did before that meaningful date: the 'template' of races, as Alexander calls it, still exists and is applied and safeguarded by the state.[6]

Let us explore a little further the manner in which we create 'facts' in the social world, one of those facts being the existence of races. This fact makes its presence felt first through socialisation and signification, the slow and complex processes of learning specific sets of meaning about the world that we encounter as we grow up. Race is a social construct. To call races social constructs means that we reproduce and maintain race as a valid category through our own socialisation, our own agency in common sense-making. This despite the scientific trashing the term 'race' has received; despite the moral and reasoned rejection of the notion through international agreements; despite knowledge of the horrors inflicted by some on other human beings, because they had been grouped as despised races. We are directly, even if not always consciously, involved in constructing and reconstructing the existence of races.[7]

In general terms, we use a conceptual scheme around the idea of race to select and interpret what we find in the world about us. It guides our sense-making. A scheme or template operates in the first instance to confirm, and to filter out whatever denies or questions, the ideas we apply in our sense-making framework. Stereotyping in general works in this way, and survives intact through confirmation, but also through continuously filtering out and blinkering against counter-evidence. We need the conceptual scheme to locate the vocabulary that allows facts to be 'constituted' into narratives of attitudes, expectations and behaviours. We also need the 'principles of significance', which allow us to sort and relate phenomena in the social world.[8]

* * *

Without socialisation into an already categorised social world, everyday life would be near-impossible to navigate. How would I know the correct response, unless I already 'know' that the world, or at least my world, consists of races, that races have different skin colours, that they look different in other ways as well, that they are not the same as I am, that they act and think differently from me, that at least some of them speak in different accents, and that all of this matters. Personally, I knew of the world of differences, even if not of races, from the moment I started being introduced into the social space that allowed me to experience life, first among my family, and then as I became conscious of the ever-widening context around me. The social meanings of my family, notions of what exists already shared within the family, of all the people and structures around me (of school, church, community), tied me to a network of meanings, a vocabulary of 'facts' about the world, that allowed and, indeed, forced me to make sense of myself and everything I saw around me in specific ways.

There was, initially, no questioning of these meanings. Because that is the way everything we experience in our 'normal lives' is – just common sense. I have already discussed such processes of gaining sense-making knowledge as signification, socialisation, stereotyping, representation and labelling. They all refer to ways in which we learn everyday behaviours and acquire the facts that inform and justify those actions, ultimately in order to make sense of the world into which we have been born and in which we have to learn the 'facts of life' as they already exist – the prior vocabulary. So we can say now that it is not a matter of being 'born with' a certain knowledge, although we may experience it as such, but of being 'born into' it. Of those processes of learning that teach us the 'facts of life', it is racialisation that is most important to my discussion, and racialism (race thinking) the inevitable outcome of this process.

Central to these processes of learning race is classification. How does this work, this way in which we create a classified world, or accept the names already given to groups already established, accept the reality as found? How are the categories into which the world seems to fit so neatly constructed? Part of the answer lies in the fact that they were already there. We have, in the course of our evolution as humans, developed an ability to think in ideas, rather than just in descriptive terms, in our approach to grouping what are otherwise perceived as a multitude of discrete items in the material world. This faculty has allowed us to formulate and cognitively integrate notions about that material world, notions that are independent of the many individually distinct forms in which they exist – notions such as 'birds' or 'taxis' or 'races'.

The recognition of the value of classification, and the application of this system of organising knowledge about the world, dependent as it is on abstract thinking, have become the essence of how modern societies work. This is the process that Zygmunt Bauman described as being 'one of the modern mind's principal powers'. Industrialised, interlinked and controlled mass societies such as those we live in now would not have come into being but for the abstract thinking and systems of classification evolved over centuries by individuals who wanted to 'bring order' to the multiplicity of living and non-living things they encountered in their world.

While immense power for good comes from abstract thinking and from classification and standardisation of knowledge, at the same time, when applied to humans (and, of course, to non-human animals), these intellectual tools hold the potential of 'categorial murder', in Bauman's words.[9] How does that happen? Essentially, classification demands that we look beyond the individual items, beyond the potentially distracting focus on the discrete elements that fall into the class. We place these items in categories and establish the standards that need to be met by those items falling into each class, each category of things.[10]

What, then, when it comes to humans? How is human standardisation ensured, where it is said to matter? Do humans also become things, interchangeable once standardised? Can the distinctive individuals disappear within the category? With all systems of classification, there is a point where the agency of the classifiers is the key factor: the decisions made by those people doing the classification, and the criteria they use for allocating individual items to each category; and then the validation or rejection of their decisions by those who ensure 'quality control' of the items in each category. With humans, as with manufactured goods, classifiers undertake the work of placing individuals in groups according to standards: these can be laid down in law, in common sense passed from one generation to the next, in the statements and interpretations of leaders of groups (religious, political, ethnic, traditional) and so on.

Classification rests on abstraction. Bauman continues his discussion of abstraction and the resulting practice of categorisation as follows:

> When [the intellectual power to abstract and classify is] applied to humans, that power means effacing the face: whatever marks remain of the face serve as badges of membership, the signs of belonging to a category, and the fate meted out to the owner of the face is nothing more yet nothing less either than the treatment reserved for the *category* of which the owner of the face is but a *specimen*.[11]

Where does this lead, where may it end up, if the individual no longer has a face, has lost her individuality, and is seen simply, terrifyingly, as a specimen of a category? Obviously, if that category is held in high regard within the power relations in any given society, the individual will also benefit, without question as to their suitability to be valued so highly, often without the need to prove their worth – to belong is enough to deserve the benefit. However, what if the categorisation is negative, shaped by those who have the power so to categorise, shaped because they benefit?

Bauman continues: 'The overall effect of abstraction is that rules routinely followed in personal interaction, ethical rules most prominent among them, do not interfere where the handling of a category is concerned, including every entity classified into that category just on account of having been so classified.' We might have sympathy for the individual, the one we recognise as a fellow human, the one we know.

However, even that personal knowledge is fragile, in each moment; we swiftly recognise the 'outsider' from our vantage point within the crowd of 'us', especially when there is a leadership that confirms the deserved extraneousness of the outsider. The personal relationship is lost, ethical treatment suspended, if we apply to individuals what we believe of the group. We see that loss in the shocked comment of the man who had just experienced in May 2013 what it meant to be 'different' from those among whom he lived in a South African community: 'They are my neighbours. Now they burn down my shop.'[12]

In certain historical circumstances it has not always been easy to efface individuals of the wrong classification; at other times already existing distance and suspicion have made it easy to ignore 'ethical rules' that would apply if dealing with one's 'own kind'. Any individual caught up in such a system is no longer asked '*who* are you?', but told 'I know *what* you are' – and treated accordingly. Ethical concerns, compassion, appreciation of the complexity of the social world and shared humanity do not feature. If we can understand the processes that lead to 'categorial murder', then we come closer to understanding that it is the *category* that is being obliterated in each case, for all its members bear equal complicity, simply through being included. And each one has no choice, no argument, no possibility of pleas for mercy based on the argument 'I was not like that' or the question 'Have you not made a mistake?'

There is hardly ever totally neutral classification of human beings, value-free and purely descriptive. Rather, classification of humans into 'us' and 'them' implies that what *we* are, *they* are not. And because categorisation fixes an 'us' and a 'them', it implies that a category of 'traitor' has to exist, to be applied to those who act against – that is, 'betray' – the values claimed, overtly or implicitly, to belong to 'us'. If there is 'beautiful', then there is 'ugly'. Labelling, ridicule and expulsion are among the mildest forms of censure of those deemed to have betrayed the essential characteristics of the group, whether it be defined in terms of national, ethnic, race or sexual categories. However, murders of lesbians and gay men, and homophobic statements at the highest levels of society in South Africa, well illustrate what can be meted out to transgressors, as does the xenophobic violence that characterises moments of local-level crisis in the country.

It becomes important to understand who defines and polices the standards that have to apply to members of each category. Classifications, and their implied or deliberately created and monitored standards, are embedded in institutions or, as Neville Alexander puts it, in the 'templates' created by the state.[13] What is required for this classificatory system to work is that there be 'agreed upon' rules for how categories are identified and labelled – or, in the social context with which I am dealing, that there be no large-scale disagreement that races exist, in the form that is required.

Melissa Nobles, who has investigated the changing use of race categories in the US and Brazilian censuses, notes the same effect in both countries, namely that an 'illusion of ordinariness' is the 'precursor of institutionalisation', such that categorisations and characterisations become part of repeated official practices within the societies where they are used.[14] Bureaucratic practices become commonsense activities. Richard Jenkins comments: 'choices are narrowed to the point where many courses of action and ways of doing things do not have to be chosen at all ... there is no need for every situation to be perpetually encountered and defined again'.[15] Such repetition is, after all, a central characteristic of bureaucracies and of the common sense of everyday life.

We live in a world where the 'banality' of race thinking is everywhere. Race has been thoroughly naturalised, it is so 'obvious' to us, that it seems to invite no questions. I owe the clearest illustration of this point to Michael Billig's book *Banal Nationalism*, which has given much content to my own explorations of the continuation of race thinking and race practice. Billig, a social psychologist, uses the concept of 'banality' to explain the depth of nationalist fervour that can be drawn on 'in times of need' through its continuous, but inconspicuous, prior presence. It is the banality that closes us off from even noticing its insidious sedimentation in everyday life, before the moment of need arises when it serves the purpose of making sense and justifying behaviour of the inconsequential kind or of the most horrendous nature against other categories of people – whether it be warfare or genocide.

The 'metonymic image of banal nationalism is not a flag which is being consciously waved with fervent passion; it is the flag hanging unnoticed on the public building', writes Billig.[16] Similarly, race thinking is not the racist incident, but is present in the sports pages, in speeches, in forms required by a very wide range of bureaucracies, in descriptions, in police training, in literature, in our everyday cognition. Melissa Nobles's reference to the 'illusion of ordinariness' that race thinking achieves in the way in which we categorise the people around us is another way of expressing that banality – the flag of race hangs limply everywhere; we hardly notice it, and are really disturbed only when it is waved with hatred.

Because we are born into a society, the ways in which the past lives on are crucial to identify and acknowledge. This legacy is located in the language we use and the weight that words carry in narrating our stories of everyday life. Many words that reflect stereotyping of people can be found in daily discourse. For example, Michael Billig writes that his argument about 'banal nationalism suggests that nationhood is near the surface of contemporary life. If this is correct, then routinely familiar habits of language will be continuously acting as reminders of nationhood.'[17] Such 'routinely familiar habits of language', in this case relating to race, were extended and fixed in many ways under apartheid, though they already reflected a prior vocabulary that was in place by 1948.

The legacy of race wounds all those who are forced to live within its categories. These are deep psychological scars that need to be acknowledged in ways that address the past, as it continues to be experienced in the present. But the acknowledgement should be accompanied by a clear view of a future in which such categories are no longer present, and their absence rewarded by another perspective of social being. The presence, and sometimes the manipulation, of such scars means that in this case the contemporary use of the deep-rooted language of apartheid remains 'obvious'.

The apartheid legacy, like any legacy of race-related discrimination and racism, goes beyond language and emotional scars. It is present much more crudely – in your face, so to speak – in the material effects of past discrimination, in the spheres of education, poverty, inequality, employment, spatial location and so on. This is so despite the fact that, in a society where global integration means that everyone shares or is expected to share the same cultural and economic reference points, a common lifestyle has been created for those who have escaped apartheid's allocations and discriminations. The massive racialised inequalities of the past and present are now approximating normality, the norm of all capitalist societies. It is just taking us time to recognise the widespread sameness of the global consumerism we are living out in South Africa. Under such 'deracialised capitalism', class will again be the first port of call in seeking to understand the growth of inequality. Race will no longer obscure the economic processes that drive this growth, and race will no longer protect those who exploit, no matter what their colour. Class conflict will take centre stage, as the vocabulary used to classify groups whose lives are so materially different from one another, and used to explain these differences, shifts from race to class categories. But as the beneficiaries of South Africa's post-apartheid deracialisation of capitalism try to obscure this shift, race scapegoating and race mobilisation will remain a dangerously attractive political resource.

We have to deal with the past, improve and debate our understanding of it, in order to make sense of the present and shape and direct our agency towards a different future. It is not an either/or approach that is required, but one that explores the past in its complexity, with reference to both race and class. We desperately need new critical approaches that address the legacies of that past, without relying on arguments that we can engage with it only by taking race, or class, seriously. In the South African context it would seem impossible if both did not feature, along with the intricate articulation of many other dimensions of this country's history and present society, such as gender and 'tradition'. We need to understand the apartheid past so as to arrive at a better understanding of the race legacy with which we must grapple.

* * *

What was the essence of apartheid? How deeply have the scars, structures and practices of that period of South African history remained in what has been attempted since 1994? Answers to these questions, if we can provide them, may give some content to the 'legacies' claimed for that period, and to an exploration of the manner in which they need to be addressed. Was the reflection undertaken during the transitional period of the early 1990s thorough and honest enough to allow South Africans to imagine achieving a truly post-apartheid country, and to gain the understanding needed for its realisation? I would argue that this was not the case, and has not been so since 1994, leaving unanswered the question of how a truly post-apartheid South Africa should be envisaged.

It is important to bear in mind that the apartheid system of racial classification did not emerge overnight in 1948, but had already evolved in the preceding decades. It was the already 'commonsense' use of race categories to separate and label groups of people that allowed the new, post-1948 race terms to establish their meaning in people's minds, to confirm what they had already learnt to accept as categories of difference. In the period after 1948, the National Party government undertook a 'refinement' of the large, inclusive and simplistic race categories already in existence, producing an overlay of ethnic (specifically cultural) categories that provided further justification for the separation of people. These ethnic categories enabled the disaggregation of the large numbers of individuals who fitted each race category as earlier defined ('Christian' and 'heathen', 'settler' and 'native', 'European' and 'non-European', 'propertied' and 'propertyless', 'white' and 'non-white', 'white' and 'black', 'civilised' and 'uncivilised', 'modern' and 'traditional'), and thus redefined the 'majority' groups – of which the apartheid (minority-ruled) state was fearful – into smaller numbers of people. Ethnicity was used to dilute race (biologically conceived in the first instance) with the notion of cultural differentiation: this made for a politicised ethnicity. But the basic infrastructure underlying these ethnic entities remained race. Apartheid was founded on the uncontested acceptance of all South Africans as members of one of a number of discrete race groups, and on an ongoing process of racialised class formation, with capitalism as the driving force of enrichment and a massively skewed distribution of wealth.

In the wider society, confirmation and intensification of an already racialised society were given new bureaucratic force, extending to just about every area of social life imaginable. For the political, social and economic infrastructure of the country to be based on 'race' demanded that race categories be subject to classification in a formal way. The Population Registration Act (No. 30 of 1950) allowed for every inhabitant of the country to be entered into a register as a member of a 'race'; for such information to be recorded in an identity document (a 'pass' for black people); and for that record of race to be used to enforce the vast array of intended consequences of race classification.

Yvonne Erasmus has researched apartheid classification procedures, which adjusted the world to be created through the application of the Population Registration Act. She identifies the distinguishing features of South African apartheid race classification, in comparison with such countries as Brazil, Australia and the southern states of the US, as 'the scale …; the extended period … (41 years); and the level of bureaucratic regulation involved'.[18] As her research indicates, apartheid classifiers experienced difficulties which arose, primarily, 'as a result of mixture between the groups that had taken place prior to the start of official classifications under the Population Registration Act in 1950'. This Act started off by stipulating three categories, later adding 'Indian and Asian' as a sub-category of 'Coloured'. Erasmus summarises the 'three main racial groups', and 'the procedures for classifying and reclassifying the South African population', as follows: '"White"; "Native" (renamed "Bantu" then "Black"); and "Coloured" (later subdivided into seven subgroups: "Cape Coloured"; "Malay"; "Griqua"; "Chinese"; "Indian"; "Other Asiatic"; and "Other Coloured"), using three classificatory criteria: appearance, acceptance and descent.'[19] By 1958, altogether 52,598 problem cases arising in the course of the first classification under the Act had been dealt with, but nearly 100,000 remained.

It was along the borders of these categories that the greatest confusion – and, hence, absurdity, misery and tragedy – was created. There, on the *skeidslyn* (the dividing line), and where the borders were crossed by individuals who refused to abide by all the restrictions that accompanied the labels, the horror of race classification was felt most personally and intimately. These cases were documented in the annual *Survey of Race Relations* and other publications of the South African Institute of Race Relations, and the dispassionate words employed reflect the absurdity, but hide the human misery of each case. The effects were there for all to see, if they were so inclined. Here, for example, are condensed extracts from one report, selected at random:

> the Minister of the Interior said that, altogether, 1,157 objections had been made to racial classification ... Classifications that were determined by appeal boards totalled 530, of which 39 went on further appeal to the Supreme Court. Of these 530 objections, 330 were upheld, and 200 dismissed.
>
> Asked about reclassifications made during 1968, the Minister gave the following information:
> Reclassified from 'White to Coloured' 3
> Reclassified from 'Coloured to White' 69
> Reclassified from 'Bantu to Coloured' 17.[20]

With regard to the consequences of such classification in terms of the act, it was noted:

In many of the smaller towns, particularly in the Transvaal, there are few Coloured people, and the authorities have provided no separate housing schemes for them. Many of them have lived their lives in the African townships ... The Department of Planning stated that an inter-departmental committee had completed an examination of the possibility of reclassifying such of these people as had become Africanized. Questioned about this matter, the Minister of Planning said that 'at this stage no action is contemplated'.[21]

So a person's race could be changed, if the individuals who so desired, for reasons of access to better life resources or because of love and personal affiliations, were willing to go through the degrading process of appeal against their existing classification and could bear refusal.

Yvonne Erasmus's research focus is on reclassification, both the extent of this practice and what it tells us about notions of race under apartheid. She notes that the apartheid government's intention was 'that everyone would eventually be classified into a single category [among several stipulated], and that this could never change'.[22] However, unless 'inter-breeding' could be prevented (retrospectively as well, it would seem) this was doomed to failure, and reclassification would remain a necessary option. This was further problematised through the mixture of social and biological interpretations of race, the former flexible to a degree and allowing for lifestyles and acceptance within a community of people, the latter indicating 'scientific' notions of biological separation. In addition the Act allowed, in certain limited circumstances, simple human agency in making decisions as to what applicants wished to be. Consequently, 'apartheid's quasi-racial population groups inevitably became inherently flexible concepts.'[23]

Some of Erasmus's conclusions are useful to bear in mind when considering the use of race categories in post-1994 South Africa, the subject of Chapter 2 of this book. For example, she found that 'race was not operationalized in the same way over the 41-year period'; nor was it applied in the same way by 'each of the actors (state, legislature, individuals) or tribunals (Boards and Courts)'; and, additionally, 'there existed no single interpretation of race over the course of this history', informed as it was by both 'science and common sense'.[24] She notes, of the trends in classification over 41 years, that 'the government's assumption that it was possible to classify the entire country into distinct population group categories ... was therefore flawed'.[25]

Erasmus's discussion of the complex role of science in classification is also important for an examination of the contemporary content of the 'common sense' employed by the multitude of present-day classifiers who place individuals in different race categories for statistical, administrative and other purposes. Descent, for example, features in classification today, as it did at times under apartheid when it overrode common sense, which would have drawn on appearance in the first instance.[26] You might look 'white', but if one of your parents was classified Coloured, that is what you would be. Erasmus specifically refers to the importance of 'the existence of a number of commonsenses' and the manner in which they were drawn upon. This means that several aspects, assumed to signify a specific race, would in various mixes feature in convincing the individual classifier of a decision – accent, dress, hair type, residential address and so on. She adds that her data 'also illustrated a way in which commonsense operated – namely through a learnt and performative nature', such as through accent and changing appearance to conform to classifiers' expectations of what each race should sound and look like – another point to which I return in relation to the status of self-classification in the post-1994 period.[27]

The effects of this formalisation of race were extensive: sex between races, spatial location, political activity, travel beyond and within the country's borders, citizenship, sport, religion, curfews and so much more could now be legislated in terms of which races were given or refused the right to move, socialise, love, work and generally exist with dignity as free human beings in South Africa. While there were intended consequences of these measures relating to the control of political and economic power, they also produced effects in the fabric of social and individual life that were impossible to foresee and impossible to measure, then as now. Relationships, of whatever kind, that existed between people of what were now different registered races were ended or massively restricted, with emotional, social and political implications that are difficult to recount adequately in the present. The ether of race and race discrimination within which all South Africans of a certain age today were raised has left a legacy that is truly impossible to address appropriately and effectively, even if its full extent can be acknowledged. At the time, the existence of races, the notion of race, was accepted by nearly all in South Africa – not only by the beneficiaries of racial oppression, but also by significant organisations within the broad resistance movement to apartheid and by people in their everyday lives. The consequences of race classification for the oppressed were dramatic, and would shape the mobilising strategies for resistance in the dominant liberation movement for years to come.

As we have seen, apartheid's adaptation of what was already present in colonial South Africa – racialised perspectives, legislation and policies – came in the form of further divisions. A clear black majority, experiencing similar forms of exploitation and discrimination throughout the country, had to be divided, to prevent this shared experience from leading to shared mobilisation by a cohesive majority against a 'minority' oppressor group. The National Party's response to this danger was the creation of ethnically defined 'self-governing' bantustans. Arguing that the bantustan policy was in line with United Nations calls for decolonisation and the granting of independence to most colonies in Africa, the apartheid government initiated the process of creating what were presented as 'national' entities that would ultimately become 'independent states'. The 'nations' of these nation-states were to be composed of ethnically distinct *volkere* (nations or peoples), identified on the basis of shared language (signifier of a generally assumed cultural distinction from other groups). No longer was South Africa to be composed of a white minority government and a black excluded majority in the same nation-state, but of 'nations' of more or less equal minority status, with white people but one such group, and each group 'entitled to' its own territory.

It was important, however, that the bantustan policy should not remove black South Africans from availability for work in the mining, farming, industrial and domestic sectors of the economy in the 'non-bantustan' regions of the country. To give effect to the post-1948 policy, without in any way harming the supply of migrant labour – the foundation of capitalist development in the region – black people were allowed into areas designated for whites only as long as they were there to meet the labour needs of white-owned industry, agriculture and commerce. Beyond that, the 'surplus people' would be forced back to 'their' 'homelands'.[28] The policy also maintained ethnic governing structures ('traditional authority'), strengthening the power of men in general and 'traditional leaders' specifically, as well as 'traditional cultures and practices' which suited both the apartheid policy and those privileged within a patriarchal value system that located itself in unchanging and neatly divided cultures.

The legacies of apartheid, therefore, cannot be reduced solely to race discrimination and the many consequential inequalities that flowed from this. Capitalism, and capitalist exploitation and inequality, did not evolve in South Africa as a consequence of racism or race discrimination, even if the benefits and the exploitation were, in effect, racially maldistributed. The racial and racist order in South Africa was structured to support the system of capitalist exploitation that took root and expanded rapidly in the nineteenth and early twentieth centuries, as was the maintenance, with various adaptations over time, of 'traditional authority' in 'traditional areas'. And this capitalist system, intertwined with maintained traditionalism, is as much a legacy of the apartheid era as the system of racial classification. It is essential that both of these legacies be addressed, if we are serious in our commitment to the creation of a democratic society. This point needs to be stressed, because at the time of the transition to democracy, and from 1994 on, capitalism as a system became part of the 'commonsense' understanding of how South Africa was and should continue to be structured, in order to enable the previously oppressed and exploited 'masses of the people' to find their place in the economic sun of a democratic dispensation.

Apartheid as a system of oppression has been misread, whether deliberately or unintentionally, by those who claim to have vanquished it. A simplified version of what it was, defined in effect solely in terms of race-based oppression and discrimination, was a necessary corollary to the simplification of the purpose of 'the struggle' as one aimed at achieving race equality – the National Democratic Revolution (NDR), in some versions as a first stage. Such reductionism, and the racialised organisational strategies employed by the ANC for most of its existence, have had consequences for the present – especially in the way the past is understood and strategies for rectifying its injustices are conceived. Such a dominant focus is astonishing, if one takes account of the inclusion of trade unions and a communist party in alliance with the nationalist movement, the ANC.

Despite claims made for an ANC-led tradition of 'non-racialism' – of a refusal to use race categories in formulating visions and principles of struggle – the evidence is feeble and the contradictions many. Opposition to apartheid in South Africa was largely directed at the obnoxious consequences of policies based on race, rather than on any informed and large-scale rejection of race as a valid category of human distinction.

The most significant example of this ambivalent relationship between resistance to race-based oppression and acceptance of race categories is

41

contained in the Freedom Charter, the document to which the ANC and its allied organisations continue to refer as the core statement of their values and vision. The Charter confirmed its adherents' commitment to an inclusive South Africa, a valuable counter to the oft-repeated demands by some resistance groups for an Africa without settlers and a radical alternative if weighed against apartheid's dream in the 1950s. And yet, the Freedom Charter is threaded through with affirmations of the existence of race and of race groups into which South Africans can be classified:

> The rights of the people shall be the same, regardless of race, colour or sex; ...
> There shall be equal status in the bodies of state, in the courts and in the schools for all national groups and races; ...
> All national groups shall be protected by law against insults to their race and national pride; ...
> Men and women of all races shall receive equal pay for equal work ...[29]

The ANC has argued that there were organisational and pragmatic reasons for the multiracialism that characterised its organisational form for most of the hundred years of its existence, and that the strategies of mobilising people on the basis of their race classification was not, ultimately, inconsistent with a commitment to building a non-racial democratic society. Elsewhere, I have indicated my scepticism about the claims made for the organisation's 'unbreakable' commitment to non-racialism.[30] But even if it is accepted that the Freedom Charter does not give voice to a clear vision of non-racialism, there can be found in its declarations a direct and principled commitment against using 'race' as a basis for governing a free society and allocating resources to its citizens, and to the creation of a future inclusive, democratic South Africa.

During the apartheid era there was, across the spectrum of resistance organisations, ongoing contestation about the necessity of relying on the race categories of the apartheid system to mobilise people and formulate a political vision for the country. There were, for example, those who refused to accept the commonsense reality of divisions between races. The Unity Movement, largely based in the Cape, provided a consistent and principled example of the rejection of race and ethnicity as other than instruments of oppression.[31] Here the analytical and principled voice of Neville Alexander stood out well into the twenty-first century.[32]

In the late 1960s, black students at some universities reacted to the impossibility of becoming involved in a truly non-racial way in the National Union of South African Students (NUSAS). Under the inspirational leadership of Steve Biko, students on some of the university campuses set aside for 'non-whites' decided to form a separate organisation, the South African Students' Organisation (SASO), formally launched in 1969.[33] At the time, what I found meaningful in Biko's writing was the variety of ways in which he explained his commitment to Black Consciousness as the essential site of resistance in a totally divided and racist society, and argued that strengthening Black Consciousness was a necessary step towards the goal of an inclusive and non-racial South Africa. Xolela Mangcu describes Biko's understanding of the relationship between Black Consciousness and a non-racial future society in the following way:

> Steve thus avoided an either/or racial politics and advocated a both/and accommodative political culture and a mature citizenship that was not afraid to confront the contradictions involved in building a national identity. He believed that black people were sufficiently 'innovative' to build what he constantly referred to as 'the open society': 'I think what we need in our society is the power by us blacks to innovate – we have the very system from which we can expand, from which we can innovate, to say this is what we believe, accept, or not accept.'[34]

Beyond politically mobilised resistance of this kind, there was also and always the resistance of daily life, of individuals who refused to live within the terms of their 'specimen status'. Nat Nakasa, a journalist in the 1960s, described such a life in an article published under the title 'It's difficult to decide my identity'.[35] Nakasa was motivated to tackle this issue by a complaint from a Dr LE Beyers to the SABC, the state broadcaster, and the Afrikaans press that these media 'had elevated "kaffirs" to "Mr." and "Mrs." instead of keeping savages in their place'. Nakasa commended Beyers for being 'honest', and hoped that they would both be around when television arrived, at which point Nakasa would 'volunteer to be used by the good doctor as a sample of a young savage'. While waiting for television, however, he said that Beyers's words had got him thinking, and gave examples drawn from the society in which he lived to demonstrate the gross racial hierarchy that existed. His reflection on his own identity, which he did not define with reference to race and ethnic classification, confronted the various identities he was meant to hold within the South African system:

> I am more impressionable than most people I know. I am the sort that speaks like an American after meeting one or like an Englishman after interviewing a peer.
>
> I am supposed to be a Pondo, but I don't even know the language of that tribe. I was brought up in a Zulu-speaking home, my mother being a Zulu. Yet I can no longer think in Zulu because that language cannot cope with the demands of our day ...
>
> I have never owned an assegai ... or any of those magnificent Zulu shields. Neither do I propose to be in tribal wear when I go to the U.S. this year for my scholarship. I am just not a tribesman, whether I like it or not. I am, inescapably, a part of the city slums, the factory machines and our beloved shebeens ...
>
> I am not even sure I could claim to be African. For if I were, then I should surely share my identity with West Africans and other Africans ... Yet it happens to be true that I am more at home with an Afrikaner than with a West African ...
>
> I don't see that there is any justification in calling me a non-European either. That is as silly as this business of South African Whites who insist they are Europeans. Some of them have never set foot in Europe. Nor did their grandfathers.
>
> It is the insistence of the whites that they are 'Europeans' which has, in part, inspired such silly slogans as 'Africa for the Africans' ... This city [Johannesburg] will never be Black or White. Black men cannot look at the tall buildings and say 'this is ours' without being fraudulent. Nor can the Whites.
>
> If I am right therein lies my identity. I am a South African like Dr. L.E. Beyers. 'My people' are South Africans ... They are a part of me. So is Dr. Beyers inescapably a part of me. And I refuse to think that part of Dr. Beyers is a 'savage'.

The fact that Nakasa could express this view, with a sense that it would be recognised and understood by at least some of his readers, is an example of the possibilities for creating a non-racial understanding of what it meant to be a South African then evolving in the country, outside the boundaries of the political discourses of the time. It is a sense of possibilities that we need to revive in our own time.

PART TWO

Prologue
Convolutes of race thinking

In 1927, the German philosopher and social critic Walter Benjamin started work on what was then to be a newspaper article on the arcades in nineteenth-century Paris, precursors in some way to twentieth-century supermarkets, department stores and, especially, shopping malls.[1] These arcades were described in an 1852 'guidebook' as 'inner boulevards ... glass-roofed, marble-paneled corridors extending through whole blocks of buildings ... Lining both sides ... are the most elegant shops, so that such an arcade is a city, a world in miniature.'[2]

The project which Benjamin undertook expanded magnificently over the next ten years or so, and took on the form in which it was left at his death in 1940. In the words of the translators of *The Arcades Project*, Benjamin held that the characteristics, the 'collective dream' of the nineteenth century, could be 'realized only indirectly, through "cunning"', through sifting through the '"refuse" and "detritus" of history, the half-concealed, variegated traces of the daily life of "the collective"'.[3] That is, at least, how he described it initially during the long process that ended with his suicide in 1940 while fleeing into Spain from Nazi-occupied France.

After the first couple of years in the life of the 'arcades project', his work was interrupted; when he returned to it in 1934, the 'scope of the undertaking, the volume of material collected, [assumed] epic proportions, and no less epic was the interminability of the task'. Most of the results of his endeavours 'remained in the form of several hundred notes and reflections of various length, which Benjamin revised and grouped in sheaves, or "convolutes", according to a host of topics'.[4] The translators conclude: 'The organized masses of historical objects – the particular items of Benjamin's display (drafts and excerpts) – together give rise to "a world of secret affinities", and each separate article in the collection, each entry, was to constitute a "magic encyclopaedia" of the epoch from which it derived.'[5]

JM Coetzee, in a review of *The Arcades Project*, describes the essence of this method as follows:

> Underlying [Benjamin's] project of getting at the truth of our times is an ideal he found expressed in Goethe: to set out the facts in such a way that the facts will be their own theory. The Arcades book, whatever our verdict on it – ruin, failure, impossible project – suggests a new way of writing about a civilization, using its rubbish as materials rather than its artworks: history from below rather than from above.[6]

What Benjamin did with the material he had collected gave me an idea about how to bring into the present argument the mass of fragments, the 'rubbish', the 'secret affinities', the 'ashes of historical objects' I have assembled as evidence of race thinking in South African society. Since before the transition to democracy, I have collected newspaper cuttings in which race featured in the coverage of specific events or people or reflections on current affairs, or where the term 'race' or variants, such as 'non-racialism' or 'racism', or one of the categories derived from it (such as 'black' or 'Indian', or 'population groups' or 'ethnic groups') appeared in the text.[7] These clippings deal not only with the despicable incidents illustrating living in racist or racialised South Africa, but also with the perpetual signalling of race existence. This second element is less noticed, because it is the language in which sense is made, the 'magic encyclopaedia', to use Benjamin's term. Even though my cuttings were gathered from only a few newspapers, and do not – and could not – cover every instance in which race featured in an article, the amount of paper that has accumulated is extremely depressing as a cumulative indicator of the times in which they were gathered.

What is the point of such a 'magic encyclopaedia'? In my case, it indicates, without an analysis of any of the individual items, simply in their numerous existence, that in the extent to which race thinking and race practice feature in the discourses of news reports and public conversation, they permeate every moment of our daily lives. It is not only that our racialised being is directly illustrated, and hence reinforced, in these reports, but that they also reflect decisions by those involved in the media industry to define their subject matter in racialised terms.

Furthermore, nearly every mention of race, in post-1994 South Africa, refers to or implies the legislated existence of race – for example, in reports about black economic empowerment (BEE) and employment equity (EE) – and the consequent need for race-based classification. And articles on topics such as BEE and EE should, but won't, tacitly remind the reader that thousands upon thousands of individuals are involved daily in the race classification of fellow South Africans or in checking that they have self-classified 'correctly'. The 'facts are their own theory': every news report about race-based decision-making is a 'fact' about the reality of racialism, about how South Africans understand their society, about what it means to them to bring about 'change' and 'correct the past', to 'transform'. It is this reality, this 'South African way of life' present in the daily shaping and retelling of what kind of society we are, that I discuss in this section.

Not only do BEE policies demand tacit knowledge and acknowledgement of what 'black' means in South Africa at present, but reporters also have to be aware of what the minister of sport means when he threatens that 'sports unions would get until next year to get their transformation targets in order, or the government would consider ending their international participation';[8] or when the cultural entrepreneur Mbongeni Ngema launches an attack on Indians in a song; or what the flamboyant millionaire Vivian Reddy means when he accuses the beauty queen and animal rights activist Caroline Ashworth of being a racist when she criticises the use of fireworks during Diwali celebrations.[9] Again, when the term 'demographics' is used to indicate race representation, as with 'transformation' and 'diversity', it demands prior knowledge.

The expectation that the reader or listener will understand the race terms, or partly hidden equivalents, used in media reports of all kinds is ever present. Race labels are repeated constantly when describing the most trivial or most profound events, whether or not they have any relevance to the episode being reported on. Race knowledge is required not only to read reports about national news, sport, culture and business activities, and to decode the implicit political concerns to which these race references allude, but also to read supplements to certain newspapers aimed at directly racialised readerships. The largest Sunday newspaper, the *Sunday Times*, for example, has a supplement named the *Extra,* which addresses issues that are presented as those of the

'Indian community', from news items and social pages to food sections and motor cars. Racialised minority status is deliberately maintained, in large part in terms of what is seen as a consumer ethnic-niche market. Advertising companies research markets on the basis of race, and then represent the results (sometimes crudely obvious) in the media through advertisements.

Where in the legislative framework of the government, besides the areas of employment equity and economic redress, does race classification play a role? In 2008, Lee Stone and Yvonne Erasmus undertook a project for the Centre for Critical Research on Race and Identity in which they looked at the broad picture of race and legislation. They found that race categories are required in three fields within which the state operates: 'Legislation prohibiting discrimination';[10] 'Legislation allowing/facilitating [fair] discrimination on the basis of race';[11] and 'Race as data to be collected.'[12]

It would have been surprising if the first field were absent. Apartheid operated on a foundation of continuous discrimination on the basis of race. Such a state of discriminatory affairs, and the accompanying racist practices and utterances, had to be done away with after 1994. Legislation designed to achieve this is, therefore, to be expected within a post-apartheid state. The second and the third fields, however, relate directly to the aim of this book. They are obviously intimately connected. If there are measures to act against the effects of previous discrimination, and if the unbreakable link between race and disadvantage is accepted (field two), then race forms the category of data to be collected as a measurement of success or failure (field three). A multitude of sites of allocation, checking, and measurement of race are, therefore, required, because there are very many sites within which the state acts and where it demands compliance with race-based classification. I will now explore the fields identified by Lee Stone and Yvonne Erasmus, and what occurs within them.

2

Fair discrimination

Constitution of the Republic of South Africa, 1966
9. Equality.
(1) Everyone is equal before the law and has the right to equal protection and benefit of the law.
(2) Equality includes the full and equal enjoyment of all rights and freedoms. To promote the achievement of equality, legislative and other measures designed to protect or advance persons, or categories of persons, disadvantaged by unfair discrimination may be taken.
(3) The state may not unfairly discriminate directly or indirectly against anyone on one or more grounds, including race, gender, sex, pregnancy, marital status, ethnic or social origin, colour, sexual orientation, age, disability, religion, conscience, belief, culture, language and birth.
(4) No person may unfairly discriminate directly or indirectly against anyone on one or more grounds in terms of subsection (3). National legislation must be enacted to prevent or prohibit unfair discrimination.
(5) Discrimination on one or more of the grounds listed in subsection (3) is unfair unless it is established that the discrimination is fair.[1]

The journey I have embarked on in this book began, in Part One, with the identification of the unexpected and regrettable continuation of race categorisation in South Africa since the election of the first democratic government in 1994. In Part Two, the central question I will address is why the race classification legacy of apartheid is *not* seen as an unwanted feature of an abhorrent past, but rather as a neutral bequest that can – indeed, should – be used in government initiatives to achieve social justice for all citizens. This section of the book also asks why the clear articulation of capitalism and racialism (if not racism) has been allowed to continue unchallenged and has, moreover, been further strengthened by the attachment of a positive moral imperative to capitalist economic growth, as a means to achieve 'a better life for all'.[2]

I focus on continuity between past and present approaches to race, but also acknowledge fundamental discontinuities between pre- and post-1994 South Africa. These discontinuities certainly do not constitute a revolutionary disruption of all the essential characteristics of the apartheid period, nor do they amount to the oft-claimed 'miracle' of the transition from apartheid, giving birth to a 'rainbow nation'. But their presence, the evidence they provide that there have been real and profound changes in South African society since the advent of democracy, is what challenges us to try to make sense of the somewhat unexpected continuities with apartheid practices that accompany them, and to consider their effects in the very different context where they continue to be the norm. Post-1994 South Africa is certainly not the same world as apartheid South Africa. That obvious statement draws attention to positive possibilities in the society that were unthinkable twenty-five years ago. At times, the continuities and discontinuities act in significant unison; at other times, they indicate direct contradictions. The continuities and discontinuities also have to be seen in a very different global context, where the increasing precariousness of individual life for the vast majority everywhere sits uneasily within the continuity of old and new forms of group claims that are always ready to divert attention from the real causes of hardship and find handy scapegoats. These may be ethnic, racial, national or religious; they are all rooted in the kinds of classificatory systems I have examined briefly earlier. The approach I will take to the articulation of these continuities and discontinuities tries to acknowledge their complexity, and will, in Part Three, work towards identifying alternative approaches to the present ways of dealing with the racial understanding of society carried over from the apartheid era.

In my analysis, I deliberately avoid making the easy term 'post-apartheid' my descriptor, for apartheid lives on in the form of 'legacies' such as those discussed in Chapter 1. These are frequently acknowledged, and sometimes meaningfully and impressively addressed, by those in power. At times, however, these legacies are used as simplistic excuses for the failure to deal with issues, such as youth unemployment, which are defined by officials as globally shared problems, as though that fact absolves the government of any responsibility to address them effectively.[3] At other times they function as what can only be seen as deliberately maintained continuities, on which government policies are based and which these policies aim to strengthen. To stand back, then, from the implications of 'post-apartheid' as an appropriate periodisation, in order to maintain a critically curious and open mind, I use 'post-1994' to refer to the society that has come into being in the past two decades, both to confirm the enormous achievement of the transition to democracy and to recognise changes that have created a country of a totally different type; but also to allow the continuities with the pre-1994 era as well as new concerns to be critically evaluated. Obviously, the continuity that concerns me most here is that of racialism and race classification, and the accompanying potential for racism and group violence. I do not accept the practice, common in some quarters, of referring to this continuity as 'reverse apartheid'. That approach simplifies the issue to the point of meaninglessness. It uses a cheap and shallow label to avoid examining the complexity of the role that apartheid race classification now plays. Such labelling practices often characterise political discourse in South Africa, serving to close down debate rather than challenge people to participate and interact more thoughtfully and creatively in addressing these difficult questions.

While race continues to play a role in South African society in a most regrettable way, the intentions, processes and most of the effects are quite different from those of the pre-1994 period. Most often, we do not fully understand them, leaving their consequences unexamined. Even if the fundamental assumption behind this continuity – that races exist – is the same one that underpinned apartheid race thinking, the content and practices differ markedly, and are changing in ways that would have been difficult to imagine under apartheid. The first difference that needs mention is that now it is a racialised majority – spoken about, accepted, mobilised and categorised as such – elected in a shared democracy, that is demanding and maintaining societal race thinking. This is a society that still measures the population in race terms, hence the appropriateness of these descriptors – majority and minorities.

Statistics from census results of 2011 tell us that there are at present nearly 52 million people in South Africa, just under 80 per cent of whom are black people (or 'black African'), with white and Coloured people representing some 9 per cent each, and Indian people about 2.5 per cent.[4] How does this compare with the proportions before 1948, the racialised figures NP leaders were factoring into their visions? In

1946, it was estimated that the population of the Union stood at 11.25 million, with Europeans making up 20.7 per cent, Natives 68.7 per cent, Coloureds 8.0 per cent and Asians 2.6 per cent of the total.[5] Not only the total numbers of people but the proportions of black and white people in the country have shown significant change. These figures and their implications, within the racialised social, political and economic world, are infrequently raised in debate. Misleading reporting, for example, sometimes uses *absolute* race category numbers to inaccurately indicate *proportions* of people who fall into different race categories, with major implications for how they are subsequently used in popular, policy and general political discourses. (An example would be when it is said that more black Africans are unemployed than white people, when the proportions are the relevant aspect to the argument for racialists.) Once race features, it seems that statistical methods sometimes no longer count.

What have we forgotten about and what have we remembered of apartheid? What have we never thought about, because we lived it rather than understood it? Historical memory, like personal remembering, is not innocent of manipulation, of erasure, denial, selection, partial reminders, of celebration of selected glories and some individuals, of being extremely partial, often devoid of context. We (and here, there is certainly not one 'we' involved) make the past. Usually this exercise in deliberate or innocent manipulation is undertaken in the service of the present – for the sake of understanding, making sense in retrospect, silencing other voices and histories, achieving security, expressing nostalgia, and many more social and personal reasons. And then, even more narrowly, social memory (often in the form of 'heritage' reclamation and 'tradition') functions in service of the powerful or those who wish to become powerful. We also need to remember that the bearers of memory change every day – death and birth ensure that. But the attempts of diverse interest groups are always there to instruct the next generation on what it should remember: in my own life, it was parents, school, the Dutch Reformed Church, Afrikaner politicians and military service.

It is useful at this point to refer to the work of the political scientist Göran Therborn in which he explores the functioning of ideology – the manner in which certain ideas about the place of the individual within a social context are manipulated, presented, enforced even, to reach a stage where they are accepted as the undisputed 'way things are'.[6] Memories of what has been, or supposedly has been, play a strong role in the three dimensions of shared social thinking which Therborn suggests are key to understanding ideology: the dominant ideas about what exists and what cannot exist, what is possible (and impossible), and what is good and desirable. Apartheid ideologues informed all citizens that 'races' existed; that what was desirable was good race relations, to be achieved through separate development for each ethnic component of the races found here; and that what was possible, or rather – the implied opposite – what was impossible, was to deny the potency of race belonging, to work towards a society in which race would not fundamentally matter.

The Equality Clause quoted from the Bill of Rights in the South African Constitution, in the epigraph to this chapter, does not mention race, except in relation to discrimination (fair or unfair). Nevertheless, the ideological memory of race remains unchallenged, as appropriate to understanding 'what exists' in Therborn's analysis. The Bill of Rights names the rights to which all citizens are entitled, thus creating an obligation on the state to deliver and ensure that such legitimate claims are met. If these rights are not realised, the state has to show reasons why and take steps to correct the situation. Equality is the organising principle of the clause quoted above; it is the goal towards which action is to be directed. This equality is presented as achievable through both the prevention of discrimination and the introduction of fair discrimination to correct previous discrimination (the unfair discrimination that defined state policy under apartheid). In our reading of this clause, a 'commonsense' interpretation kicks in immediately: it is assumed that 'discrimination' refers in the first instance to race discrimination (and then, secondarily, to discrimination on grounds of sex and disability). Inequality as the result of exploitation is, however, not mentioned at all; nor are the conditions under which millions of South Africans lived under the apartheid system of 'traditional authorities', trapped in rural areas as 'subjects' of 'chiefs' and 'kings'. It is a very specific and selective view of what apartheid was about that informs this compromised, but enthusiastically accepted and impressively employed, document. Without the omission of 'exploitation' from the inherited conditions that need to be rectified, the notion of a 'deracialised' capitalist order, and hence of black economic empowerment, would not have been so easily accepted as part of the new moral order. With capitalism, as a system, exonerated during the transition and subsequently, the obvious point of reference is race. But how to ensure that the capitalist system is maintained, revived, reproduced – even in a bizarre way 'deracialised'?

As we saw in Chapter 1, any social formation that relies on the notion of race, and hence race classification, for the implementation of policy has to engage the participation of thousands of bureaucrats and an even greater number of bureaucratic and policing practices, whether in the public or the private sector, to make, implement and monitor decisions relating to such classification. But beyond this, the acceptance of such a system relies centrally on the passive or active involvement of citizens in adhering to race-based policies and in 'reading' the contexts and situations they encounter in their daily lives in terms of these policies. The existence of a policy framework based on race also means actual or potential political mobilisation of people by employing notions of 'race' – the one cannot exist without the other. In examining race-related practices in post-1994 South Africa, one needs to take into account the different forms of classification that exist simultaneously: formal, legally required classification, but also the classification that happens tacitly as part of the banality of everyday common sense and unreflective socialisation. The first category includes classification imposed through the census requirements and classification required by government departments wishing to measure progress in achieving 'equity'. The second includes classification in the media, whether it be through reporting and commentary, through letters and talk shows, or in advertising and entertainment; as well as the classification present in the pervasive race thinking that shapes public and private conversations – the prior vocabularies we work with in everyday life. The content of this classificatory vocabulary has to be examined, for it is not exactly the same for every individual or every racialised group: people create and imagine their group identities, and those of others, in distinct ways.

In this chapter, I am concerned with three questions that arise from the particular ways in which the statement in the Equality Clause of the Constitution relating to discrimination – 'Discrimination on one or more of the grounds listed in subsection (3) is unfair unless it is established that the discrimination is fair' – has been interpreted in government policy since 1994: why has race classification in a post-apartheid South Africa continued as a state-driven project; how is race classification, and hence racialism, effected and ensured in post-1994 South Africa; and, finally, what are some of the consequences of this practice embedded in the 'post'-apartheid society – or, does it even matter?

POST-1994 RACE CLASSIFICATION: WHY?

There are certain sections in the Equality Clause of the Bill of Rights quoted in the epigraph that I wish to highlight. Section 2 allows the state to take necessary measures *'designed to protect or advance persons, or categories of persons, disadvantaged by unfair discrimination'*. Sections 3 and 4 prohibit discrimination, by the state or others, on a wide range of grounds, 'including race', and demand that the state legislate and act against it. Section 5, however, allows discrimination, if *'it is established that the discrimination is fair'*.

Section 2 of the clause refers to both individuals and 'categories of persons', with obvious reference to the apartheid past. Discrimination on grounds of race, ethnicity, class position, gender, sexuality, urban–rural location and religion could all be covered by the legislative intentions of the drafters of the Constitution, as all of those categories were discriminated against in some form under apartheid. Section 2 also distinguishes between 'protect' and 'advance' – it is the latter which concerns me here. This section of the Constitution forms the essential background to the argument presented below, which attempts to come to an understanding of why race classification has been retained and expanded since 1994. In the absence of any clear, politically acceptable alternative justification for the continued use of apartheid race categories in the post-1994 order, Section 2 provides an indication of the intention of this practice, namely to bring about 'equality' for all members of South African society. But it does not specify that race-based redress should be the form of action used to bring about this equality or that race-based equality should trump all other forms of equality between individuals and groups of whatever description or existence.

Pierre de Vos, professor of constitutional law, draws attention to the selection of race as the primary basis of action towards achieving an equal society. He states that 'the jurisprudence of the [Constitutional] Court is ... perhaps more complex than many would admit. First, it recognises that constitutionally valid remedial measures aimed at addressing the effects of past discrimination need not always focus on the category of race.' Can that be read as 'need not *ever* focus on the category of race', except to legislate against racism and racial discrimination? De Vos first 'loosens' remedial measures from a sole focus on race, an apparently single category with clear components, and suggests that 'where other factors could be used (and where these factors would be effective to address the past and ongoing effects of racial discrimination and racism), this would be constitutionally permissible because the group targeted need not be drawn with absolute precision'. He then adds a further point:

> because the [Constitutional] Court has signalled [that] the context in which a programme [of redress] is evaluated is all important and that the context may change as society changes, the jurisprudence also gestures at the contingent nature of present racial categories and power relations. Although the Court has not said so explicitly, the jurisprudence leaves the door open for future contestation of race-based remedial measures.[7]

Subsequently, in 2014, De Vos shifted his focus somewhat in a contribution on redress.[8] Heading his article 'Why redress measures are not racist', he defended race-based redress against such accusations, largely because of the correlation between 'race' and forms of disadvantage. My argument here is clear: race-based redress need not be racist, but there are other ways of addressing the same concerns; race-based policies fail because they deflect attention from the heart of the matter; and the use of race has consequences that cannot be controlled by defending such practices as innocuous.

And yet, even though there are other ways, debates around policies of affirmative action and black economic empowerment illustrate the all-too-obvious choice of race as the near-exclusive basis for corrective action against some of the legacies of apartheid. Except in the case of some universities debating alternative criteria for selecting students, most criticisms of this practice are based on the unfair application of existing race-based redress legislation and policies. It is not easy to shift the public discussion about redress and equality beyond a purely race-based paradigm, as the 2014 De Vos article illustrates. Even when another major category for which deliberate corrective action is needed – 'women' – is the focus of concern, race soon enters the debate and shapes that category to its liking, as I will show.

So, the demand for measures of redress can be traced fairly easily to the constitutional injunction to create an equal society, a morally and socially laudable goal. At the time of the drafting of the Bill of Rights, the 'how' was still open to analysis, interpretation and policy creation. Thereafter, however, a decision was made, or simply accepted as common sense, exclusive of other possibilities and of the negative consequences, that such a goal had to be realised through maintaining and utilising race. As a result, the governing party, the African National Congress, through the state, has ensured the continuing need to identify and classify South Africans in terms of race. Race-based redress was there from the start of the democratic period, even though the legislation enforcing race-based employment equity and black economic empowerment came several years after the 1994 transition. To mention just two confirmations: the Reconstruction and Development Programme (RDP), which was first formulated as the ANC's manifesto, carried indications of this before the first elections of April 1994; and the first census in 1996 used race categories, which were defended as essential for measuring change in a democratic society. Since those years, there has been very little sign of a discussion of alternatives, or even of 'race', on the part of the state and the governing party. As Neville Alexander clearly stated, the role of the state is essential, though not exclusive, in the perpetuation of the use of race and other categories in any society. States create social templates. Anthony Marx, in his comparative study of the practices of 'making race' in the US, Brazil and South Africa, makes the same point: 'State actions were highly consequential in shaping the template of modern race relations. Where and when states enacted formal rules of domination according to racial distinctions, racism was reinforced ... Where racial domination was not encoded by the state, issues and conflicts over race were diluted.'[9]

It is understandable that once race has been chosen by the state, or any organisation for that matter, as the main category for redress, the measures to assess success or failure will have to use the same category. Data collection, therefore, serves as another reason for race classification. It is noteworthy, however, that in its use of race as a core category the national census, the main tool for such measurement, predates the legislation giving effect to race-based redress. Race was already available as a key framework for counting and classifying the South African population – for the social scientists engaged in the task of race-based data collection at Statistics South Africa (the census bureau), and not just for the politicians for whom they were working. Although a new head was immediately appointed after the transition to democracy, many of the previous statisticians were retained for their skills. It is clear, from personal communications with people involved, that there was no real disagreement on retaining previous categories – one of the reasons being that it provided comparative continuity, as well as data within the categories that were to be used for measuring redress in future.

However, the census is not the only measure of race-based redress. Every single site where redress legislation may apply has to engage in the process of classification, because the agents at these sites need to account to another body – an internal supervisory structure or an external government agency – for the numbers of people in different race categories affected by their activities. For example, school teachers have to classify themselves and pupils, because the principal has to report on race group numbers in the school to the Department of Education, and so on up the ladder of accountability. In universities, heads of departments have to report to faculty heads, who report to human resources staff, who draw up tables and send these to the national Department of Higher Education and Training, where they are assessed. This procedure is required in all government departments, most businesses, municipalities and so on. In each case the first step is the classification of individuals employed in these structures, by themselves or by other employees.

In summary, the government's argument for the retention, re-creation and utilisation of race categories runs as follows: to correct, in the present, the effects of past race-based discrimination, measures addressing the situations of people, as they are located within specific race groups, are deemed appropriate and necessary. As the race categories fixed under apartheid formed the sole or primary basis of discrimination at that time, we, therefore, obviously need to use the same categories as measures of redress when implementing policies aimed at wiping out apartheid's legacies. Yes, we are committed to abolishing discrimination in any form, and to guarding against further discrimination, also on the grounds of race, and we are committed to the dignity of all citizens. After all, those are the values enshrined in the Constitution. However, employing race categories in order to establish a new order is not in fact discrimination, because it is fair discrimination. It is fair because, unlike the aims of apartheid policy, such race-based discrimination is aimed at achieving an equal society and not one that enforces inequality between people. Race is the clear measure of the inequality resulting from past discrimination. For this reason, fair discrimination can be required in law and in practice, as the Constitution states. New legislation and policies that discriminate fairly to advantage a specific race group or groups are morally correct, socially demanded and democratically supported. What is implied in such an argument is that there is no perceived assault on the dignity of citizens and visitors through race classification, as this would be unconstitutional.

As can be seen from this summary, the approach adopted by the present government rests on a specific understanding of apartheid, namely that race was the basis of the apartheid system, and that discrimination rather than exploitation was the root cause of the inequality that shaped the lives of the 'previously disadvantaged'. The argument relies entirely on the equation of present material disadvantage with past racial discrimination. Since all people not classified white under apartheid were discriminated against to various degrees, all people not classified white in the post-1994 order need the benefit of fair discrimination, including the right to exploit other people for material gain. In other words, extending participation in capitalism through black economic empowerment is fair discrimination. In this framework of 'redress', the intimate symbiosis of race and class, of discrimination and exploitation, in defining the nature of the apartheid beast is not acknowledged.

For example, addressing the 2009 conference of the Black Management Forum, where he was re-elected president shortly after being appointed as director-general in the national Department of Labour, Jimmy Manyi unsurprisingly rejected class-based redress measures. In an interview after the event, he told a journalist from *Rapport* newspaper that this was 'a mistaken approach. Apartheid was race-based – people were discriminated against on the basis of race skin colour.'[10] It seems that the infrequent introduction of class within any debate on redress from whatever source (government ministers, trade unions, social analysts), and of the existence of a capitalist system, occurs only (and half-heartedly) when attention is drawn to gross conspicuous consumption, or gains that came to blackness through the capitalist system and its opportunities for corruption and excess in general. These are systemic aspects, but the criticism is voiced when the system can be personalised – individuals who are corrupt, individuals who treat workers badly, individuals who flaunt their wealth gained through redress measures. In other words, criticisms of the excesses of capitalist practices among the new or the old elites are occasionally voiced by one or two cabinet members who are also senior officials in the South African Communist Party.

In terms of the logic of the current policy for addressing the inherited inequalities of apartheid, race-based measures of redress will continue until 'correct' race demographics have been achieved in every institution and economic structure, especially in the ownership of capital and the upper levels of employment in large workplaces. This argument was, for example, raised in 2007 by the chair of the Employment Equity Commission, the often-present Jimmy Manyi.[11] 'Fair discrimination' on the basis of race will continue in this way towards the impossible goal of equality. Increasingly, 'equality' is seen simply as a matter of race quantities: every race silo in every institution, in every category and level of employment, in every sports team, in companies listed on the JSE, must be filled in the same proportion of races as exists in the South African population as a whole. This is what is meant by the policies of 'affirmative action' and 'employment equity', which have come to govern many aspects of employment practices across the public and private sectors. What is also argued in effect is that because of the centrality of race-based affirmative action or employment equity, the population as a whole must of necessity be classified in terms of race identities.

South Africa remains a thoroughly racialised society, a condition which affects social actions and interactions, perceptions and analyses, institutions and their daily operations, far beyond the apparently specific areas of corrective action. To build an enormous, albeit largely invisible, system of classificatory practices, agents and monitors, and yet expect the already existing racialism and racism not to continue, seems incomprehensibly naïve, if not cynically manipulative. In the next section of this chapter, I examine post-1994 legislation and policies that have played a central role in reinforcing, and in some respects regenerating, race thinking in South Africa.

RECREATING RACE

The first level at which ideas of race are reproduced is located where deliberate and coordinated actions can be taken by the state to make citizens engage with everyday life and think in particular ways. Such state actions demand decisions, and reflect the dominant power relations represented in the state policy-making locations. The dominant ideas in a society – the ideas that 'tell us', in many and complex ways, what exists, what is good and what is possible, which we often accept with little or no question or reflection – don't just exist around us, like the air we breathe.

They – our racialised, consumerist, gendered selves – are inserted into our environment through planned actions – through, for example, public speeches by politicians about the legacies of apartheid and the need for affirmative action, in which we are addressed as members of races; or campaigns run by government departments to achieve a specific social goal such as being tested for HIV, which speak to us as sexual beings; or the massive consumer advertising campaigns and promotion of lifestyle models, with no mention of inequality or the costs of such engagement with capitalism. Of course, there is contestation, and the official ideology of the governing party and the state is often a battleground of ideas. But the majority party, as government, has the advantage of being in power and, hence, can implement its own vision through policy and legislation, through containing critical debate, through privileging certain positions, individuals or institutions, and through disseminating ways of thinking and practice.

I have drawn attention to the choices involved in selecting policy directions in order to give effect to the broad and uncontroversial mandate to implement massive post-apartheid corrective action. In this section, I will briefly deal with two seminal moments: the Reconstruction and Development Programme (RDP) in 1994, and the Growth, Employment and Redistribution strategy (GEAR) in 1996. The RDP offered approaches, albeit in contradictory fashion, that did not rest on race-based policy, but did claim to have been informed by the Freedom Charter. With GEAR the choices had already been made in this regard, and it was the economic direction that was at issue.

In the years of the liberation struggle, the ANC presented its historical 'calling' as the implementation of the vision of society embodied in the Freedom Charter. In the period leading up to the first democratic elections in 1994, the organisation formulated a more detailed policy and programme of action, the RDP, which served as its election manifesto.[12] In the introduction to the RDP, Nelson Mandela, then president of the ANC, described the document as follows:

> This document – The Reconstruction and Development Programme – is the end of one process and the beginning of another...
>
> The process now underway is that of developing the detailed policy and legislative programme necessary to implement the RDP. In preparing the document, and in taking it forward, we are building on the tradition

of the Freedom Charter. In 1955, we actively involved people and their organisations in articulating their needs and aspirations. Once again we have consulted widely.

However, in 1994 we are about to assume the responsibilities of government and must go beyond the Charter to an actual programme of government. This RDP document… represents a framework that is coherent, viable and has widespread support. The RDP was not drawn up by experts – although many, many experts have participated in that process – but by the very people that will be part of its implementation.[13]

So what signals did this 'start of a new process', this 'actual programme', give to an inclusive citizenry, before the first democratic elections? The document itself starts as follows, prefiguring the introduction to the Constitution: 'The RDP is an integrated, coherent socio-economic policy framework. It seeks to mobilise all our people and our country's resources toward the final eradication of apartheid and the building of a democratic, non-racial and non-sexist future.'[14]

In section 3.4.3.2, it is stated that the new government will 'promote the development of a unifying national culture, representing the aspirations of all South Africa's people (this cannot be imposed, but requires educating people in principles of non-racialism, non-sexism, human rights and democracy)'.[15] The commitment to non-racialism, at least as far as it informs policy execution, is mentioned a few times. In the quotation here, importantly, it asks for educating people 'in principles of non-racialism' – it is not a given, not an empty claim, but a task.

Section 1.2.7, part of answering the question 'Why do we need an RDP?', captures some of the possibility for an inclusive focus on the problems – a moment that could have been approached in a different, imaginative way, rather than the racialised route chosen:

It is this collective heritage of struggle, these common yearnings, which are our greatest strength and the RDP builds on it. At the same time the challenges facing South Africa are enormous. Only a comprehensive approach to harnessing the resources of our country can reverse the crisis created by apartheid. Only an all-round effort to harness the life experience, skills, energies and aspirations of all of the people can lay the basis for the new South Africa.

Certainly not all, black and white, would have heeded this call, but many, on a non-racial basis, would have. In the 1980s, the United Democratic Front (UDF) had provided clear evidence of that, through its approach to organising South Africans across the country in opposition to apartheid. However, along with calls for all South Africans to participate in meeting the enormous challenges left after apartheid, and the general absence of 'race' in the document, race-based approaches are proposed in specific cases, such as the judiciary: 'The judicial system must reflect society's racial and gender composition, and provide fairness and equality for all before the law.'[16] In section 4.4.6.3, the phrase 'deracialise business ownership' appears, along with three references to 'black economic empowerment'.[17] Several formulations compete at times. The 'Prisons' section is introduced with section 5.8.1: 'The staffing of the prison service must be based on non-racial and non-sexist principles. Prison staff will need to be trained to reflect this approach and to transform the present military command structure of the prison service.'[18] In the discussion of the 'Public Sector', in section 5.9.1, it is said that 'A defined quota of all new employees should come from groups that were disadvantaged on the basis of race and gender'.[19] The same section states that at the end of the century the public sector should reflect the 'national distribution in terms of race and gender'. This particular call became especially contentious after the turn of the century, as I will discuss below.

For the rest, there is a remarkable absence of race terms to speak about corrective action in such areas as water, employment, skills, housing, transport, the environment, nutrition, health services, infrastructure and dignity – exceptions include communication, the economy and agriculture/land. Far larger reference was made to poverty, people in rural areas and poor people. The document referred to 'all South Africans', 'the people', 'women' and so on as entitled to redress measures. The contrast with what would develop very soon in official discourse is striking. The section that deals directly with 'affirmative action' does not refer to race at all, but focuses on eliminating discrimination rather than measures of numerical redress.[20]

By 1996, however, as the pressures of the global economy began to tighten their grip on South Africa, the RDP had given way to a new programme of action called GEAR. This refocused government priorities away from the social goals of redressing the material ravages of apartheid on the majority of South Africans' lives, and towards making the country a competitive player in the global capitalist system. At best, the one was now seen as necessary for the other. Although the introduction of GEAR changed the location of economic thinking and policy further to the right, it did not directly address race as an issue.[21] Race-based redress may not have been confirmed through legislation as yet, but it was already firmly entrenched. The link between race and class was implied.

However, the Freedom Charter has not been totally forgotten by those who originally formed part of the ANC's support base, in the enthusiasm for much more qualified goals informed by social justice. In February 2013, for example, the Charter was invoked by the general secretary of the National Union of Metalworkers of South Africa (NUMSA), Irvin Jim, in a strong defence of policies favouring the working class and a simultaneous attack on the ANC as a government 'siding with capitalism'.[22] The most powerful union movement, the Congress of South African Trade Unions (COSATU), of which NUMSA is a key member, is one of the three organisations in the governing alliance with the ANC and the SACP. Current references to the Freedom Charter by members of the tripartite alliance serve two main purposes: to challenge and offer an alternative to government policy (and thereby to indicate that there is an ongoing ideological tussle within the alliance over the nature of its own legacy and vision), and here too NUMSA, through its general secretary Irvin Jim, offers an example. He said in December 2013 'that the ANC continued to undermine the resolutions made during its conference in Polokwane in 2007. One of these was to make COSATU, SA Communist Party (SACP) and ANC alliance a strategic centre of power.'[23]

When the ANC expresses allegiance, it is to claim the Charter as the moral framework that still informs the party, and, therefore, allows it to continue to be seen as a 'national liberation movement'. For example, party spokesperson Jackson Mthembu said in June 2013 that 'South Africans should take pride in the achievements made since the adoption of the Freedom Charter 58 years ago … "South Africa is a better place today than it was in 1994. We are on course, building the society envisaged by the representatives of the people of South Africa 58 years ago."'[24] It was reported on 5 August 2013 that the newly formed Progressive Professionals Forum (again involving Jimmy Manyi) embraced the Freedom Charter and had 'thrown its weight behind the African National Congress. This message came through loud and clear during its launch meeting.'[25]

The commitment is, however, to a path of building a new society that as far as race classification goes involves a 'fair' replication of apartheid categories. In the next two chapters, I discuss further the practices of race redress and, hence, of race classification.

3

What counts when race is at work

The ANC's race-based approach to redressing the economic legacies of apartheid has been focused largely on affirmative action measures prioritising the access of some groups of South Africans to employment and capital accumulation opportunities over others. What have not been explored clearly, in its unquestioned dominance, are the dangers of this kind of 'racial economics'.[1] This is the focus of my exploration here. There are, of course, extensive areas of redirection of spending in operation, away from apartheid's discriminatory and racist allocation of resources, areas that benefit poor people, through extending services previously exclusive to or biased towards white people, and so on. Such rationalisation, the ANC argued, would free a very large share of state expenditure and help address the inequalities in South Africa after 1994. Here, the problem lies more in the failure to implement effectively than in any lack of intent, and in vast amounts disappearing into private pockets through corruption – the most egregious cases being stealing from the poor: in service delivery, pensions, education, school feeding schemes, and the like. Infrastructural development, in general, would fall under such redirection and redistribution of state expenditure, as would health services and much of education – here, race need not be mentioned, as these actions obviously work towards a more equal (non-racial) society.

State-driven affirmative action in South Africa goes back to the early years of the Union, with the entrenchment of race-based categories of labour and of white privilege in labour legislation and employment practices generally.[2] In 1949, Sheila van der Horst summarised 'the labour market' that had been created from 1910 as follows:

> [It] has been very strongly influenced by the multi-racial character of South African society. The type and grade of work done by individuals,

70

and hence the wages earned, are determined by their racial group as much as by their individual aptitudes and preferences. On the one hand, opportunities for employment are different for different members of racial groups. On the other hand, the quality of work performed is affected by the unequal opportunities open to different groups in respect of employment, wages and living conditions in general. Capacity and willingness to work are also affected by the different educational facilities available for members of different groups.[3]

After 1948, the ruling National Party (NP) took measures to ensure that state enterprises and the civil service would show a marked preference for its white Afrikaans-speaking supporters. Dan O'Meara writes of this apartheid period:

> Shortly after assuming office in 1948, the NP government initiated a systematic purge of senior civil servants and a general reorganisation of the state bureaucracy. Pro-NP bureaucrats were promoted into senior posts, and care was taken to cosset all ranks of an increasingly Afrikanerised civil service as one of the NP's major bases of political support ...
>
> The two crucial security apparatuses of the state, the police and the military, had likewise to be brought under the firm control, not just of Afrikaners, but of reliable Afrikaners.[4]

This was ethnicity-based affirmative action, informed by political loyalty – what is now, under an ANC government, called 'cadre deployment', or the centralised allocation of party members to key positions in state bodies and in provincial and local government. The effects of the apartheid policies, adding to the dire consequences of earlier legislation, were extreme. 'By the time of the transition to democracy in 1994, it was apparent that apartheid educational and labour market policies had yielded a deeply entrenched racial gradient in unemployment, employment and wage rates.'[5] In a nutshell, here lies the need for redress or corrective action – and not only in the labour and employment field, but in the whole range of socio-economic spheres where apartheid measures had their effects.

From the start of the post-1994 period, heated, but infrequent, debate has characterised the implementation of affirmative action policy, whether this came about through moral and political pressure applied at the level of the firm or organisation, or as the result of legal requirement in terms of the Employment Equity Act (EEA) (the Act is dated 1998, but it became effective only in the early twenty-first century). This Act is best known and most often referred to, but there are several other Acts allowing race to feature: for example, the Public Service Act (1994) and the Skills Development Act (1998).[6] The issue of affirmative action and 'fair discrimination' was raised in the course of the adoption of the final Constitution in 1996, specifically because of the inclusion of the Equality Clause, although by that time race-based redress and affirmative action were firmly established, as the RDP document clearly indicates. Affirmative action, based on race categories, was generally accepted at the time, in contrast with the intense debates on procedures and quantification that were to follow after the EEA was passed. There was also at that time no real discussion of what 'affirmative' meant, beyond reference to the example of the US. The commonsense reliance on race quantification as a measure of change was a core assumption in all the debates, despite the very different histories of the two countries.

During the 1990s and early 2000s, broad private sector commitment to affirmative action, especially in large firms, was measured in terms of compliance with the stated policy of the government, and with reference to what firms and institutions generally saw as morally imperative in an inclusive society, politically necessary or economically advantageous. Later these dimensions became synonymous, as political necessity also meant economic advantage through tenders. It was reported in 1995 that 'more than 94% of companies have affirmative programmes in place, a 21% increase on last year', according to FSA-Contact Affirmative Action Monitor.[7] However, the base was so small that any claim was probably possible. More realistically, it was reported that 'the percentage of black senior managers has increased to just over 4% in 1995, and is expected to reach 9% by 1998'. White senior managers were expected to decline to 87 per cent by then. It seems that capitalists were reading the pre-EEA signs from the ANC and responding with at least verbal commitments to the race-based demands.

In the civil service, a totally different picture applied. Changes in the composition of the civil service after the first democratic elections were initially not so rapid, because of a 'sunset clause' that had been proposed by the SACP leader, Joe Slovo. This was meant to alleviate some of the fears expressed by the NP power-holders during the transitional negotiations, and was accepted by the ANC and other parties to the negotiated settlement. The clause involved 'the acceptance of a constitutionally entrenched system of power-sharing for five years after the first democratic election'.[8] No major clearing-out of the civil service was to take place with immediate effect. Over time, direct intervention and the restructuring of management in government departments led to an increase in the ratio of managers to servants from 1:700 in the 1990s to some 1:5 after 2000, and the previous ethnic preference for white Afrikaner civil servants shifted to reflect more accurately the race demographics of the country. Overall, the racial composition of the civil service changed from 60 per cent white managers, to fewer than 40 per cent by 2001, with the African component of 'generic black' managers accounting for more than 50 per cent by then.[9] It must be taken into account that in 1994, with the incorporation of the bantustans, many black civil service managers would have been taken on board. The *number* of white managers, however, increased during this period, because the total number of managerial posts shot up.[10] Vinothan Naidoo concludes that 'efforts to transform the racial composition of state bureaucracy have yielded considerable shifts in the representation of black people since 1994'.[11] Criticisms are regularly made, from within the state and from outside, of the direct and indirect costs in terms of service delivery efficiency of such restructuring in some cases.[12] As Habib and Bentley write, this is not to claim that the inefficiencies occur only because appointments are made of unqualified people, but also because vacancies are maintained when people of the required 'demographics' are not available or where the demands of restructured positions are impossible to meet.

Accusations of negative effects or practices as well as positive claims about affirmative action were frequently aired in public discourse throughout the 1990s. Opponents of the practice of affirmative action rejected it, because it was argued to be discriminatory, despite the Bill of Rights clause that allowed 'fair' discrimination. Within this argument the phrase 'reverse apartheid' was sometimes employed. Others argued, however, that the approach had negative developmental effects, most specifically in relation to tackling inequality in general, rather than that between races. This second line of argument has become much more often expressed. On the other hand, affirmative action was supported, for the obvious reason that it benefited a large number of individuals, albeit as representatives of race groups, and also because it was seen as a measure of essential redress after a period of intense discrimination. Supporters argued that changing the racial profile of the employed population would create opportunities for new and expanded skills utilisation. It was generally acknowledged that one of the signal failures of the apartheid system had been to meet the demand for skilled labour, because of job reservation policies.

Interestingly, objection to affirmative action policies on the grounds of rejection of race classification occurred only infrequently. It is clear that South Africans, and not only those in power, overwhelmingly accepted that they belong to races.

Discussion of race classification, as a necessary and deliberate state project, does not feature in public ANC policy debates, as far as I have been able to establish, before 1997. I exclude consideration of the first census after 1994: the new government seems to have accepted apartheid race classification as the basis for this demographic exercise with no public discussion at all. When race classification did appear in the media, it was at, of all places, a conference of the South African Human Rights Commission (SAHRC) in 1997. A representative of the South African Institute of Race Relations (SAIRR) reported in the Institute's journal *Fast Facts* that while some state employees who attended the SAHRC event expressed concern about 'deliberate race quotas for their personnel', for example because there were simply not enough qualified black personnel available, others, among whom were members of the SAHRC, supported deliberate classification.[13] This position had also been advanced by Lot Ndlovu, the president of the Black Management Forum, as it 'could be necessary to enforce affirmative action'. Barney Pityana, then the chairman of the SAHRC, 'said that he planned to press ahead with the HRC's proposal, made in September [1997], that every employer be required to undertake an annual "social/racism" audit with the same force as a financial audit'.[14]

By the end of the 1990s it had been decided that affirmative action, or employment equity, would be legislated. In the language of one of the major Acts aimed at achieving this ideal state of equality, the Employment Equity Act of 1998, race is to be seen as equivalent to 'previously disadvantaged' (or those previously discriminated against, along with women and disabled people).[15] This left little room for any other approach to affirmative action, except as adjuncts, subservient to the race-informed reading of social reality.[16] The Employment Equity Act reads as follows (the language of the Equality Clause in the Constitution is recognisable here):

> The purpose of this Act is to achieve equity in the workplace by:
> (a) Promoting equal opportunities and fair treatment in employment through the elimination of unfair discrimination; and
> (b) Implementing affirmative action measures to redress the disadvantages in employment experienced by designated groups in order to ensure their equitable representation in all occupational categories and levels in the workplace.

What is 'equitable' representation in terms of this Act? Is it simply 'fair and just', or is it to be interpreted in terms of the quantifiable proportional representation of groups created or maintained through race classification? And who are the 'designated groups'? The Act stipulates that this 'means black people, women and people with disabilities'. Worth noting is the use of the word 'people' in the EEA in terms like 'disabled people' and also at times 'black people', hopefully because it was accepted by the drafters of the Act that neither 'disabled' nor the generic and dehumanising term 'black' covers neatly demarcated categories of objectified human beings. The word stands out precisely because of the contrast it makes with the vocabulary that specifies race categories, with its effacing and, hence, homogenising function.

But who are 'black people'? 'Black' is used, states the EEA, 'as a generic term which means Africans, Coloured and Indians'. Whether intentionally or not, breaking down the generic black category in the Act in this manner leaves the way open for claims or practices in terms of a hierarchy of disadvantage or of power among the different apartheid-era categories of oppressed people. Categorise by race, and conflict between groups so classified is inevitable. Apartheid discovered this and benefited from it, and events in the new state provide many illustrations. And, as before 1994, such conflict involves all groups involved in a classificatory schema, and not just the obvious and expected categories 'black' and 'white'.

NATIONAL, REGIONAL OR LOCAL RACE
DEMOGRAPHICS?

The policy of economic redress at the very top, at the level of ownership and directorships, known as 'black economic empowerment' (BEE), has had a much more vigorously debated reception than the Employment Equity Act. This is not surprising, as owners of capital have far greater access to media, and because business sections in newspapers have capitalists and capitalism as their bread and butter. In 2003, the Broad-Based Black Economic Empowerment Act (No. 53) was introduced specifically to make it a requirement for public and private sector organisations to implement measures towards this end – such as favouring BEE-compliant firms to gain tenders. Here, the stakes are far higher, since the Act deals with the economic conditions of employers and owners, rather than of employees – those accumulating the profits rather than those producing them or managing their production.

The Act's intended beneficiaries have established themselves firmly in close relationship with, or even within, the state itself, nationally, provincially and locally. The increase in public attention paid to questions of redress once BEE became the focus of government policy is not surprising, as this is where new economic power lies, where wealth seems to be available for the taking, and where patronage and corruption are active in their most unfettered form. BEE has also provided extremely lucrative career paths for many of those ANC cadres and political allies previously employed in local, provincial and national government positions. The nature of the process was pointed out in 2008, for example: 'Black economic empowerment deals came under the spotlight once again with Deputy President Phumzile Mlambo-Ngcuka strongly criticising those with social connections being the only ones to benefit from the stakes.'[17] As recently as 2013, ANC cabinet members still needed to assure the general population that civil servants would not be allowed to do business with the state, and that this would be strictly monitored in future. The assurance has had to be reiterated several times, probably because few believe it. The *Financial Mail* reported:

> A new law that makes it illegal for civil servants to do business with the state was the toughest parliament has ever had to deal with because it 'treads on so many toes', says public service & administration minister

76

Lindiwe Sisulu. But this is only the beginning.

The stiff opposition that the bill came up against from civil servants during its passage through parliament paints a picture of the kind of political will it's going to take to implement it.

The bill started out as a 166-page document. It was eventually passed as a 16-page bill.

'Our approach when we had a contentious issue was to leave it out. The bill now offers the bare essentials, a framework. We hope to introduce the other issues as amendments when we have more time to negotiate them,' says Sisulu.

She says the ANC should have regulated public employee business interests from the start of its time in government. Its neglect of this means that for two decades civil servants have been allowed to do business with government. One in five South Africans works for government.

Various probes over the past five-year term provide some insight into how serious the situation really is.

The Public Service Commission estimates that misconduct and corruption by civil servants cost the country R1bn last year. The 2013 losses represented a tenfold increase in three years …

The department of basic education also revealed how the 3000 department employees who were found to have done business with it during the 2010/2011 and 2011/2012 financial years earned R152m. Of these employees, 2485 were teachers.[18]

Politics and capitalism in South Africa, as elsewhere, have always articulated with each other in a complex process. They continue to do so now that questions of socio-economic redress form part of the government's agenda. This is partly because of the dominant position occupied by the ANC, an organisation straddling a deliberately unclear line between party, liberation movement, voice of all people other than reactionary anti-revolutionaries, route for the advancement of 'cadres', and the state itself. An added dimension is the all-encompassing race-representational role – or, rather, mission – that the ANC claims for itself: political, cultural, economic, historical. Inevitably, this produces a 'redress' agenda in which correct race allocation and party-political connections frequently ensure enrichment for individuals. William Gumede has captured well the current state of affairs:

Run-away corruption and the service-delivery problems besetting the country are the result of a country governed by conflicting systems of governance. On the one hand there is the official system: the Constitution, resting on a clear democratic-value framework. On the other there is the ANC's unofficial system of governance: the party's liberation ideology framework, which is supposed also to be supported by a democratic value system.[19]

The problem is aggravated, argues Gumede, because the ANC's system of values has become rotten, though it is still seen by many ANC comrades as elevated above the Constitution, the justice system and such state agencies as the Public Protector. A fascinating illustration can be found in the lead-up to elections in 2014 when the ANC claimed support from the Christian God and from 'traditional ancestors'. It was said that the ANC would win the elections in 2014, because 'God is with us'; and it was also claimed that the ANC would rule until 'Jesus comes back'.[20] A continuity with Afrikaner claims of being divinely inspired?

The ANC is the leading component in the tripartite alliance, with COSATU and the SACP, and holds the majority of seats in parliament on its behalf. Tensions over issues of class and race are to be expected in debates within the alliance, though when compromise positions are reached in parliament and in policy formulation processes it is always the ANC's pro-capitalism and pro-BEE positions that carry the day. Both the trade unionists and the communists have voiced strong opposition to the direction taken in BEE policy, which they view as a spawning ground for new capitalists where skin colour can be used by individuals to gain access to and advantage within the capitalist class. However, neither COSATU nor the SACP has raised any objection to race-based policies in general, or at least not visibly in public. As members of the alliance, trade unionists and communists are drawn into parliament and cabinet, where their contributions are mostly indistinguishable from purely ANC members. Such silence is surprising, as South African communists were often in the forefront of the drive within the liberation movement as a whole to evolve organisational practices based on non-racialism. Moreover, the formation of new trade unions in the 1970s occurred under the banner and practice of non-racialism and under conditions extremely hostile to such a commitment.

Of course, there are challenges every now and then to these

affirmative action and black economic empowerment policies, though they do not involve questioning the validity of race itself, but rather the consequences of favouring one race group over another. Nor is capitalism even mentioned; it is simply another given. A recent case serves well to illustrate how a certain interpretation of race-based redress is perceived in the arena of employment equity. Although it has, in fact, been the basis of implementation for some time, certain high-profile challenges have recently brought it to widespread public attention and evoked disbelief and criticism. This apparently controversial interpretation of 'employment equity' rests, in essence, on a reading of equity as measured by the 'accurate' representation of all four of the apartheid-era race groups, in the same proportions as exist in the racially categorised national population (according to the census), in every employment context where pressure can be exerted by the state. This measure – usually expressed as 'correct demographics' – is not an aberration. It, in fact, informs all 'targets' set by government for employment equity, within its own departments and agencies as well as in the private sector for large national companies.

The implications of this legislative goal are hardly ever acknowledged: first, that national race demographics must already exist (the census ensures that); which in turns means that someone must know that there are races and be able to recognise them (census enumerators, for example, are given information in this regard); that the appropriate and correct race categories in the South African situation have been identified (continuity with apartheid will provide the answer here); and that the data exist to indicate how many members of each race group are where, at whatever level and place of employment (agents, in their thousands, are required to participate in providing such data by classifying people in their employment context). Within this framework, a further question arises: does each workplace and firm have to reflect local, provincial or national race demographics, among workers, managers and owners?

In the colonial, segregation and apartheid eras, the spread of the population in South Africa was massively determined by where people moved, or were forcibly moved, or prevented from moving. In the twentieth century, the legal frameworks for population location and relocation were created through such measures as the 1913 Land Act, the 1950 Group Areas Act and the various Acts that established the bantustans. In addition, the National Party government declared the

Cape Province a 'Coloured preference area' through a policy directive issued by the Bantu Administration Board in 1982.[21] This meant that the flow of 'bantu/black people' into the province would be prevented or at least dramatically reduced, and jobs provided instead to people classified Coloured.[22] Black South Africans 'illegally' in the region, having come from the 'independent' bantustans of Ciskei and Transkei mainly, 'were deported ... in terms of the Admission of Persons to the Republic Act', based on the section of this Act that was 'normally used for deporting unwanted non-South African criminals'.[23] As a result of this policy, by the time of the first democratic elections the proportion of people classified Coloured in the Cape Province (thereafter subdivided into the Western Cape, Eastern Cape and Northern Cape) was substantially greater than in other provinces. It is also of relevance that, since the elections of 2009, the Western Cape has become the only province controlled by the opposition Democratic Alliance (DA) – an understandable thorn in the flesh of the ANC and an ongoing challenge to its claim to represent all South Africans discriminated against under apartheid. This is the context for the recent controversy that has erupted over implementation of the Employment Equity Act.

Jimmy Manyi, then director-general of the Department of Labour, contentiously raised the issue of equity based on provincial versus national race figures when he appeared on the television programme *Robinson Regstreeks* (Robinson Directly) on KykNET on 9 March 2010. He made the case for national race demographics to apply in the Western Cape.[24] Manyi has been controversial at times, but he has also been highly influential in giving voice to many black people's demand for inclusion in the formal economy as owners or senior managers, rather than just as employees (where affirmative action policies and the EEA would set the framework for their advancement, rather than BEE legislation).

It was, however, as director-general, the most senior official in the department most directly concerned with the implementation of official employment equity policies, that Manyi created probably the most intense controversy and stirred debate with the greatest impact on 'race relations' policy in South Africa to date. In his appearance on the television talk show, he made the following statement:

> Let me just make some key comments on the last discussion about Coloured people. I think it is very important for Coloured people in this

country to understand that South Africa belongs to them in totality, and not just Western Cape. So this over-concentration of Coloureds in the Western Cape is not working for them… They should spread in the rest of the country. There is a requirement of Coloureds in Limpopo, there is a requirement of Coloureds everywhere else in the country. So they must stop this over-concentration situation because they are in over-supply where they are. So you must look into the country and see where you can meet the supply. And also… let's understand that this Employment Equity Act is a very good Act in the country.

Whatever was Manyi referring to? The important word here is 'requirement', referring to the need for every employer to aim at the 'correct' race demographics. He was not, in the first instance, referring to skills unique to people classified as Coloured, but rather to the specimens of a category of people labelled Coloured, and he implied that failure of these people to 'spread' throughout the country as employees in the 'correct' proportion relative to national demographics did or could carry penalties in various forms. Table 3.1 illustrates his concerns. It clearly shows that, at least at the time of the 1996 census, the Western Cape's racial silo for Coloureds was too full, and that for African/ Black was relatively empty. Manyi did not mention Indians, whose 'disproportionate' presence in KwaZulu-Natal also offends, but not as much as African/Black, a category in oversupply there.

But the table also shows that there is not a province in the whole country that has the ideal race demographic mix in this apartheid-like approach. The moment one race is present in the 'correct' proportion, another is out of kilter – disturbing the race planners' ideal. Apartheid manipulators had a field day with tables and maps such as these. They acted on their abstract calculations, policing and, often viciously, removing those located where the grand scheme did not allow for them, being surplus to the requirements of capital and state ideology, 'black spots' on the vision of a white canvas.[25] In contrast, Manyi post-1994 is 'asking' Coloured people as members of a social group to correct their maldistribution themselves, with the implicit warning that if they do not do so there will be no employment or promotion opportunities for them in their home provinces.

To make this unfortunate historical mess easier to understand, let us look at provincial percentages, compared with the national 'demographics'

3.1 Number of people in each province by population group, October 1996

	Eastern Cape	Free State	Gauteng	KwaZulu-Natal	Mpuma-langa	Northern Cape	Northern Province	North West	Western Cape	South Africa
African/ Black	5,448,495	2,223,940	5,147,444	6,880,652	2,497,834	278,633	4,765,255	3,058,686	826,691	31,127,631
Coloured	468,532	79,038	278,692	117,951	20,283	435,368	7,821	46,652	2,146,109	3,600,446
Indian/ Asian	19,356	2,805	161,289	790,813	13,083	2,268	5,510	10,097	40,376	1,045,596
White	330,294	316,459	1,702,343	558,182	253,392	111,844	117,878	222,755	821,551	4,434,697
Un-specified/ Other	35,849	11,262	58,654	69,423	16,120	12,208	32,904	16,635	122,148	375,204
Total	6,302,525	2,633,504	7,348,423	8,417,021	2,800,711	840,321	4,929,368	3,354,825	3,956,875	40,583,573

Source: http://www.statssa.gov.za/census01/census96/HTML/CIB/Population/25.htm, table 2.5, accessed 18 September 2012.
Note: Northern Province is now called Limpopo.

(in the final column of Table 3.2). Here, it is obvious to anyone that, once race categories are accepted, Coloured people should be 8.9 per cent of the population in all provinces, and certainly not 54.2 per cent in the Western Cape and 0.2 per cent in what was then Northern Province (now Limpopo). Indian people should be 2.6 per cent everywhere, and not 9.4 per cent in KwaZulu-Natal and 0.1 per cent in Free State. The complications of these proportions become even more an affront to the vision of national demographic equity if we take local (municipal) 'racial spread' into account, which I won't do.

It was only when the TV interview with Manyi was aired, and was uploaded on YouTube on 24 February 2011, that the debate erupted with vehemence.[26] What were to be the 'demographics' to be used in setting employment equity targets, and against which criteria would progress be measured and penalties imposed? It must be noted that in the South African context the word 'demographics', at least in the press and public debate, nearly always refers to 'race representivity' – that is, whether there are the correct proportions, relative to the national census, of black Africans, Coloureds, Indians and whites in the specific site at issue. This can be a workplace, government office or classroom, or the country's employment profile as a whole – and then at every level of appointment within the employment hierarchy in each case.

Manyi's statement came after a long period in which government

3.2 Percentage of the population in South Africa by population group, October 1996

	Eastern Cape	Free State	Gauteng	KwaZulu-Natal	Mpuma-langa	Northern Cape	Northern Province	North West	Western Cape	South Africa
African/ Black	86.4	84.4	70.0	81.7	89.2	33.2	96.7	91.2	20.9	76.7
Coloured	7.4	3.0	3.8	1.4	0.7	51.8	0.2	1.4	54.2	8.9
Indian/ Asian	0.3	0.1	2.2	9.4	0.5	0.3	0.1	0.3	1.0	2.6
White	5.2	12.0	23.2	6.6	9.0	13.3	2.4	6.6	20.8	10.9
Unspecified/ Other	0.6	0.4	0.8	0.8	0.6	1.5	0.7	0.5	3.1	0.9
Total	100.0	100.0	100.0	100.0	100.0	100.0	100.0	100.0	100.0	100.0

Source: http://www.statssa.gov.za/census01/census96/HTML/CIB/Population/26.
htm, table 2.6, accessed 18 September 2012.
Note: Northern Province is now called Limpopo.

pressure to implement affirmative action policies had been felt by the business sector. During this time private and public sector employers had evolved their own interpretations of what such action should entail, and of appropriate 'demographic' targets for the composition of their workforce. For example, a human resources officer from a big banking group told students in a class I was teaching in the mid-1990s that the bank applied branch-level demographics when setting its affirmative action targets. Consequently, if a branch was deemed to be in an 'Indian area', then Indians would be the majority employed at that branch (in these cases selection by language ability could easily have made non-racial sense). In 2000 the eThekwini (Durban) metro council said: 'It is not council policy to consider only one race group ... There is no quota system, but we have certain targets. Eventually an organisation such as ours will have to reflect the demographic profile of the province.'[27]

In 2004, a statement from the public affairs director at the University of KwaZulu-Natal (UKZN) at the time, Dasarath Chetty, seemed to indicate that 'national demographics' applied in selection criteria at the university's medical school, which (as with all medical schools) has racial quotas – under apartheid legislation separate medical schools were created for specified races. Chetty said that 'as far as health professionals go, and in relation to the size of the different population groups, Africans are severely under-represented'.[28] While the setting of targets or quotas was left up to the various universities with medical schools, the Department of Higher Education made it clear in 2002 that intervention would ensure compliance: 'while the Ministry is reluctant to set quotas, because of the difficulties in setting realistic targets, it would not hesitate to introduce quotas "if institutions do not develop their own race, gender and disability equity targets and put in place clear strategies for achieving them".'[29] In 2014, just before the elections in May, the minister of communications, Yunus Carrim, spoke to potential voters and informed them, in an aside, that there were too many Indian doctors and that parents should tell their children to follow a different route in their ambitions and studies.[30] Racially selective admissions policies, especially at the universities of KwaZulu-Natal and Cape Town, have made news often, and at UCT their implementation stimulated debate and research on race-based affirmative action and alternatives in useful ways, even if not to the satisfaction of all participants.[31] How the state will respond to these initiatives remains the crucial question.

The issue of the 'appropriate demographics' to be used in setting affirmative action and employment equity targets continues to be debated, or avoided, with no clear statement on the matter emerging from national government. Nevertheless, Mildred Oliphant, when minister of labour, may have provided an indication of the official government position on the matter in 2012 when she reported on both private and public sector success in making progress towards racialised equity targets, using the evaluative Report of the Commission for Employment Equity. According to a newspaper report, the minister 'said the Western Cape was the worst performing province in terms of race "at nearly every occupational level", and among the worst performing in relation to black women'.[32] The newspaper report added: 'Both national and regional demographics had been used during the formulation of the report, Labour Department chief director Thembinkosi Mkalipi said, since employers were required by law to consider both when they recruited employees. National demographics had been used to evaluate national government departments and provincial demographics to access [sic] provincial departments or private workplaces, he said.'

With the clarification from the minister of labour in mind, let me return briefly to the Western Cape and one government department in particular, Correctional Services (the prisons department). Several people employed in the Department of Correctional Services in the Western Cape had been negatively affected by the policy of applying 'national demographics' when making staff appointments and promotions. It became clear during the process of appeal to the courts by Coloured warders affected by fair discrimination policies that what had been attributed to Jimmy Manyi as his individual view was, in fact, the official Department of Labour policy on how the generic category 'black' was to be interpreted. It referred to a hierarchy of disadvantage, based on the race categories African, Coloured and Indian, with Africans being the most disadvantaged and, therefore, first in line for any employment or promotion possibilities.[33]

Manyi's various pronouncements and claims were rarely challenged from within the ANC. One of the few exceptions needs mention. Ben Turok, the ANC struggle veteran and member of parliament, wrote an open letter on 18 March 2011, from which I quote:

> I suggest that Manyi be given a piece of land in the Kalahari to start his own community of ethnically pure Africans, diluted with the exact proportion of other races in what we would call 'Blackistan'.
>
> He could get good advice from Orania [the right-wing white separatist town in the Northern Cape] on how to manage the project.
>
> I am beginning to believe that black chauvinism is the last refuge of scoundrels like Jimmy who have no place in our movement or government.
>
> Maybe the former members of the Indian Congress, the Coloured People's Organisation and the Congress of Democrats, together with our real African comrades, should give our views on how we build a non-racial South Africa.[34]

Of interest is that Turok did not sign as an ANC member, but went back to the 1950s and 1960s to show where he drew his inspiration from: 'Ben Turok (in my capacity as former National Secretary of the Congress of Democrats)'.

The Department of Correctional Services stated, when a Labour Court ruling went against them, that 'the department stands its ground in using national demographics in its equity plan'.[35] The judge had gone to the heart of the matter when he said that the race of the applicant, a Coloured man, 'had been an "insuperable obstacle to his appointment"' to the post, where he was working in an 'acting' capacity in any case. The argument of the department was that, because of his classification as a Coloured (in the past and the present), he was not a member of a race that had been the most discriminated against under apartheid and, furthermore, that he was of a race that was over-represented in the Western Cape – where he and his family had lived all their lives. That is what underlies the hierarchy of discrimination within the 'generic black' category in the EEA, and hence the need for 'national [race] demographic representation'.

The issue of national demographics and the implications for Coloured employees, especially in state departments, had been brewing since early 2012, during the Manyi affair. Selection of apprentices and promotions, to take two instances, followed what were national rather than provincial race distributions. In May 2012, it was reported that Advocate Dumisa Ntsebeza would 'lead a team to investigate the Department of Correctional Services' employment equity legislation targeted only at the Western Cape'. The minister of correctional services made the announcement. This followed 'a complaint by a group of coloured officials within the Western Cape department of correctional services earlier this year'. The officers had 'threatened to take the department to court after they were overlooked for promotions in favour of their African colleagues'. The officers said that in the Western Cape, 'where coloureds are in the majority, [the department] should have applied provincial instead of national demographics'.[36] Whether the Ntsebeza investigation took place or not, the officers did go to court, providing evidence of exclusion from promotion due to the application of national race figures. Dumisa Ntsebeza appeared for the state in the case that followed. The predictable response during 2013 was growing calls on 'Colouredness' and 'own interests', and counter-calls against divisions. The Western Cape political veteran Peter Marais formed a Bruin Bemagtigingsbeweging (Brown Empowerment Movement).[37]

In October 2013, the Cape Town Labour Court ruled in favour of Solidarity (the trade union movement that brought the case for the prison officers) and the affected Coloured correctional services officials, and against government departments and ministers.[38] The judgment referred to an earlier employment equity plan (EEP) (in place during 2006–2009), which clearly set national race demographic targets (for example, 8.8 per cent for 'the coloured population'). The judgment noted:

> The EEP contains tables relating to employment equity targets at various levels of the workforce. The tables are explained, for example, in the following notes:

'At level 3 only Whites and Indians should be appointed. At salary level 4 only 9 African males, one African female and one Coloured male need to be appointed to balance representation of the workforce. At level 5 only African females, Whites and Indians can be appointed.

'At level 13 African males stand at 63 with a gap of –9 which indicates no African male should be appointed. 24 African females, 4 Coloured females and 1 Indian female need to be appointed at this level.

'At level 14 only 3 African females and 1 white female need be appointed.'

The judge concluded: 'I have found that the individual applicants who are black employees in terms of the EEA have suffered unfair discrimination in that the selection process utilised to decide on their application for appointment to various posts was premised on the understanding that regional demographics do not have to be taken into account in setting targets at all occupational levels of the workforce in DCS.' For my focus, it must be noted that race classification was not at issue, but rather constitutional principles and their application in further legislation, in this case the EEA. It is inevitable that the underlying problems will remain, with consequences that are identified here.

Like so many other cases in recent years that have been brought to the courts by employees or their representative organisations on grounds of 'unfair discrimination', the Western Cape correctional services case made it clear that not only does the EEA require race classification and acceptance of the classified status by all concerned (including the judge), but it also has the effect of evoking racialised responses to what is perceived as unfair discrimination against the group. This results in group-based political actions driven by the argument that, for example, 'coloured people have to organise as coloured people because they are treated as coloured people'. So the process continues, reinforcing itself in a feedback loop.[39] The social theorist and activist Neville Alexander, referring to cases such as these, where minority status is claimed and forms the basis of opposition to the state and, in effect, to another race group, pointed out the dangers – here he was referring to the Bruin Belange-Inisiatief (Brown Interests Initiative).[40] While accepting cultural differences, he warned that 'to form a national organisation in order to promote the interests of a group defined by "race", besides the fact that it is probably unconstitutional, is highly dangerous because of its exclusivity'.[41]

87

As Adam and Moodley have remarked, 'the funeral of formal apartheid has been accompanied by the increasing legitimacy of ethno-racialism'.[42] The term 'ethno-racialism' is an accurate one, for what is being referred to is usually the divisive categories of language-based ethnic groups, which were recognised under apartheid in order to divide the majority.[43] We need to investigate more fully the intertwined issues of ethnic mobilisation, racialised minorities and claims made under the rubric of 'tradition', especially how 'fair' and 'unfair' discrimination in terms of these categories articulates with racialism more broadly and with gender discrimination.[44] The negative effects of these group identities are most strongly experienced by girls and women. John Comaroff and Jean Comaroff also draw attention to another aspect of the perpetuation of group identities based on ethnicity and tradition, namely the presence of 'an ethnic economy', capitalising on cultural differences in South Africa. An inevitable consequence of this is that people start to see their economic security and prospects as tied to membership of an ethnic group or acceptance of their status as 'subjects' of a traditional leader.[45]

From this discussion of race demographics and their regionally specific application, we can draw several conclusions. The first is that all citizens have now been told, very directly, that where they live in South Africa as a racialised individual, and hence as a specimen of a race group, has implications for where they may find employment or promotion. The implications of this, even if only as a threat of what is possible, ripple through all aspects of people's working lives: options for children's schooling, the employment situation of one's partner, property ownership, free choice of where to live, and so on. The government's 'clarification' of Manyi's statement indicates that this applies not only to 'non-designated' people (white men, in other words), but to members of every one of the race categories. It also extends to gender categories – white women have also been found to be in oversupply in certain cases where the broad category of 'women' is entitled to benefit from fair discrimination in terms of the EEA. I will return to this aspect of the demographic hierarchy later in the chapter.

The second conclusion is that the debate about these issues takes place with a prior acceptance that there *are* race groups, that they can be recognised in the appearance of individuals, and that their existence makes (common) sense to all. The debate about affirmative action and economic redress is, therefore, part of the process of confirming and reproducing race thinking. The applicants in the correctional services case were not contesting race. What was at issue was not race classification but the consequences of being allocated to one or other race category, which in this case, it was claimed, overstepped the mark in moral and economic terms.

A third important aspect of such processes of discrimination based on race demography is their complete dehumanisation of individuals and the total lack of concern by government for the implications these policies can have for individuals. How could Manyi (to use him here as an example) be so deaf to his echo of apartheid callousness in speaking of oversupplied groups? Whether such dehumanisation is unintentional or not, whether the policy's aim is justified as morally correct or not, it is the effect on the classifier and on the classified that is inevitable. Race belonging cannot be avoided. The individual is trapped in the already classified body, burdened with the allocated attributes of his or her category. The moment of reflection, of doubt, of curiosity, of acceptance of shared humanity, of interacting with an individual rather than a specimen, has been removed, long before the occasion when race classification or the acceptance of category membership is required. The event can be as mild as an everyday social interaction or as vicious as a xenophobic or racist attack. Most commonly, at a formal and deliberate level, it is in the workplace or place of study.

The same effect was present in the implementation of apartheid policies when, for example, the term 'surplus people' was used to justify the forced removal from 'white South Africa' of people classified as Native/Bantu/Black, or the allocation of people to their own 'group area'. The treatment of individuals as interchangeable specimens of a category is the first step on a path that can, and does, lead to abuses and atrocities of all kinds.[46]

HOW BLACK ARE THE CHINESE?

A case that revealed far more about state approaches to issues of race and citizenship than those in power might have desired was the challenge by the Chinese Association of South Africa (CASA) to the exclusion of Chinese South Africans from the EEA category of 'previously disadvantaged' individuals. As in the 'demographically correct proportions' case involving the prisons department, race classification and allocation were at the heart of this case; here, however, it was an insignificant minority group (in terms of absolute numbers) that was affected. The challenge by CASA raised the issue of what happens when the criterion for being a beneficiary of Acts such as the EEA is met, namely having been previously discriminated against under apartheid, but when the racialised criterion is not.

The matter can be stated as follows: Chinese South Africans, always a very small minority in the country, were discriminated against until 1994 as members of one of the several 'non-white' population groups defined by apartheid legislation as subsections of Coloured. CASA applied to the Pretoria High Court, after seven years of attempting to resolve the issue with state departments and even parliament, for recognition of their 'previously discriminated against' status in terms of the EEA and BBBEE Act, as well as confirmation of this ethnic group as full citizens of post-1994 South Africa.

Two main issues were at stake from the perspective of CASA: direct benefits through inclusion under affirmative action and black economic empowerment legislation; and recognition of their dignity as full citizens of a democratic South Africa. They were accepted as meeting the requirements for such status in 2008 after the Pretoria High Court decided in their favour, in a case that was initially opposed by the state. They were then placed, by the court, within the category 'generic black', since under apartheid they had been allocated to the Coloured race group, which now also fell within this umbrella 'generic' category. Such an allocation well captures the contradictions of directly equating race with discrimination and exploitation: generic black = previously discriminated against (even if not directly exploited in all cases); generic black includes all those falling outside the white category under the 1950 Population Registration Act; hence, people of Chinese origin should have been included in 'generic black' as part of being Coloured. But, the EEA, while referring to Coloured, did not specify 'as used under apartheid' (whereas the census takers did).

This decision, of including the Chinese as among those 'previously discriminated against', was greeted publicly with derision or resentment in many quarters. For example, it was reported that some black business people described it as 'surprising, irrational, shallow, opportunistic and inexplicable', and remarked that 'we as blacks should jealously guard that we were historically disadvantaged under apartheid'.[47] Some of these responses were comments on the absurdity of post-1994 race classification; many also captured the fragility of social cohesion in South Africa at the very time when the worst single manifestation of xenophobic violence since 1994 had recently taken place. There were plainly racist and resentful comments from some of those already classified 'black' who were aiming to benefit from such status, especially from individuals whose voices were often heard in various media. Even the minister of labour, Membathisi Mdladlana, despite having withdrawn initial legal opposition to the CASA court application, greeted the court's decision with 'baffling statements such as: "What I know is that Coloureds don't speak Chinese"... Perhaps revealing his true feelings about the court order and his lack of understanding of the essence of the case, he also commented: "I suppose if I stand up now and say I want to be classified as pink, so maybe a court will agree that you are pink, even if you are not pink."'[48]

If ever there was an official confirmation that the legislation was not based on the clear and inclusive goal of equality for all, but on race as the essence of post-apartheid society and of all measures of redress, this was one. Yvonne Erasmus and Yoon Jung Park note that while 'Chinese' were deemed to be Coloured under apartheid, lack of definition of the terms in post-1994 legislation means that in effect 'purified' notions of who belongs to the present categories operate behind the scenes.[49]

In Yoon Park's exploration of this tragic and frightening case of race classification, she notes that 'in South Africa, where such identifications and official classifications come attached to resources, contracts, jobs and promotions, confusion surrounding racial classification becomes politicised and highly contested'.[50] It is because these 'confusions' are uncommon, given the effective racialisation of social interaction that exists in the population as a whole, that the case of the Chinese South Africans reveals so much – if and only if we get round to raising the questions, of course.

HIERARCHIES OF DISADVANTAGE: RACE TRUMPS ALL

Further confusion arises when hierarchies are introduced within, for example, 'generic' race categories (black), a specified race category

(Coloured) or another category of 'previously disadvantaged' (women), for the very reason that these categories come with opportunities and power, as well as disadvantage. It is worth noting at this point that the hierarchies of previous disadvantage, and hence of race, are a big step back from the solidarity of 'black' demanded by Black Consciousness organisations from the late 1960s. Inserting the umbrella category 'generic black' into the legislation has left the door wide open for racialised levels of previous disadvantage – and, therefore, degrees of redress – to be identified, claimed and applied. In the case of women, no component parts are indicated in the EEA, but these are then introduced via the racial hierarchy within which women are further classified as members of race groups. (We could imagine, in this Alice in Wonderland world, that such divisions could be introduced within the category 'disabled', but as this category is very far off the 'demographic representation' mark, such divisions have not been mooted.) Simply put, the race-based affirmative action argument is that there are too many white women and too few black women employed in South African workplaces, especially at the top levels where it matters most in terms of salaries and decision-making power.

The issue was raised in 2006, when the newspaper columnist Vuyo Jack noted that white women were absent from mention in both the BBBEE Act as well as in the Codes of Practice that flow from them (for the obvious reason that they were not 'black').[51] However, they were there as part of the designated category 'women' in the EEA. He noted two sides of the debate. On the one hand, sex differences in ownership categories remain (men in general, and men in each race category, overwhelmingly dominate control of capital), indicating extensive discrimination against women in daily practice and in the implementation of policy; but, on the other hand, 'white women were not discriminated against through any specific legislation' (in the apartheid order, although Jack did not mention that few would challenge the definition of South Africa, then and now, as an extremely patriarchal and sexist society). The rest of the article dealt with this conundrum and provided statistics showing white women's failure to achieve equal status with white men, women's failure to achieve equal representation with any men, and black women's location at the bottom of the ladder of continuing discrimination in the workplace at the higher levels, compared with men and other-raced women. Jack ended by calling for every effort to be made 'to ensure that black women are integrated into the mainstream economy', but that white women, as a raced and sexed category, should be counted even if not benefiting directly from affirmative action: 'The bottom line is that what gets measured gets done, and if there is no measure of how white women and disabled people are progressing in the economy nothing will be done to empower them.' Jack's accurate statement reflects part of the problem as well, though. Numbers are what count, while the ultimate intention gets lost. As Appadurai and others have warned, the numbers are not neutral: 'As abstractions produced by census techniques and liberal proceduralism, majorities can always be mobilized to think that they are in danger of becoming *minor* (culturally or numerically) and to fear that minorities, conversely, can easily become *major*.'[52]

In the year after Jack's article appeared, the Commission for Employment Equity (CEE), in a report submitted by its chairman, Jimmy Manyi, to the minister of labour, suggested that there should be a 'sunset clause' for affirmative action for white women.[53] The suggestion came because while there was a '"meagre and shocking" 9.5%' rise for black people in top management, white women's presence at this level had increased by 4.5 per cent to 14 per cent, or 'more than three times the economically active population in that particular group [indicating further hair-splitting in category-making]'. Manyi said white women were 'seriously over-represented'. The minister, however, felt the 'designated' status of white women should remain. Two months later, the Black Management Forum (BMF), of which Jimmy Manyi was also president at the time, submitted a call to the parliamentary portfolio committee on labour to remove white women from EEA designation.

More debate followed, with *Rapport* editorialising that such exclusions because of over-representation of a category make sense, but that what was more important was the dramatic skills shortages in the country.[54] Writing in the *Sunday Times* in the same month, Mamphela Ramphele, activist, businesswoman and former vice-chancellor of UCT and World Bank director, praised corrective action measures in general, but added more complexity to the discussion, by referring to other data that indicated the extent of 'intra-race' sex inequalities: according to her, white women made up only 15 per cent of the white category of top management, and black women a mere 7 per cent of the black top management category. She also raised a longer-term concern about the social aim of corrective action, reminding readers of the ultimate purpose of redress in whatever form:

a focus on 'redress' of past wrongs without a holistic view of desired goals risks making the whole empowerment process a compensatory mechanism for past wrongs rather than a mechanism for the creation of an equal opportunity climate for all citizens. A compensatory model carries the danger of rewarding people with senior positions without an adequate performance framework that enables – as well as demands – that they demonstrate the value they bring to the prosperity of the country.

Ramphele's argument, therefore, was that while a 'holistic approach to "sunset clauses" is essential ... targeting white women at this stage would send a terrible punitive message that would undermine our widely lauded transformation process'.[55]

The BMF responded to Ramphele a week later in a letter to the *Sunday Times (BT)* with an attack on 'celebrity black women' who did not support the call for the removal of white women from inclusion in a designated group.[56] A year later, further calls were made for the exclusion of white women from the legislation, largely on the basis that they had 'not been discriminated against under apartheid' (and yet were benefiting disproportionally).[57] These were made by Dianne Schneider, a partner in the accounting firm Deloitte and Touche, with support from Gugu Maloi, the founder of Iman Africa, Anneke Potgieter, a financial manager at Suncoast Casino, and Sindi Koyana, the president of African Women Chartered Accountants. In the simplified version referred to by these women and used in law, 'discrimination' was restricted to the effects of apartheid race-legislation: here, there was no accounting for exploitation, or sexism and patriarchy. The category 'women' existed only in racialised subdivisions.

These arguments illustrate how a fixation with both numbers and race categories imposes restrictions on public debate and thinking about questions of social transformation and efficient service delivery. In consequence, gender discrimination, in part the motivation for the EEA, is not even mentioned, and the overall goal of creating a new country that benefits all is lost sight of in the predictable point-scoring exercises which the debates have become. And in these debates, race trumps all, and numbers are the measure of success or failure. In effect, the logic of the argument for basing affirmative action on race criteria leads to the assertion that white women were not discriminated against under apartheid, while bantustan leaders and ethnic police and military forces were.

RACE FOR SOME OR MERIT FOR ALL?

A last point on the implications of a race-based approach to redress in the workplace is that employment equity applies to the end-point of a process that starts even before primary school (at birth) and in conditions of disadvantage in which the majority of South Africans still find themselves. Before the effects of employment equity and economic empowerment kick in for any individual, there is a 'pipeline' of nearly two decades in operation. I refer not only to the obvious point that all children are introduced to race categories as soon as they engage with any aspect of society, but that schooling should prepare those who will benefit from being the first choice in any employment selection process based purely on merit, regardless of whether they belong to any 'designated' category. Unfortunately, far too few gain the skills to meet the minimum requirements of any job, even those that allow them to be fairly discriminated in favour of. Enormous gaps exist for preschool and school children, depending on class, gender and location, gaps that are increasingly acknowledged. Inequality starts at birth.

But at the point of entry into tertiary education institutions, such a history is mostly ignored. End-point evaluation, where quantification measures 'transformation' success, does not address the need to improve the quality of preschool, primary and secondary education. No wonder there are not enough previously – and still – disadvantaged young people to compete against their presently advantaged peers. How many schools have functioning laboratories, dedicated teachers, flush toilets, never mind electricity and computers? In the case of 'women' as a designated group, the over-representation of white women in top managerial positions is 'blamed' on the privileged education these women are assumed to have received, rather than on the failure of education for the overwhelming majority of South Africans.

What is the 'supply chain', to use that inadequate term, that ends up failing to meet the needs of South African children as well as the demands of the economy by concerning itself only with 'quantity control' and 'fair discrimination' at the top? What dimensions of meaningful redress and affirmative action are ignored through the near-exclusive focus on the numbers game of race-based quotas or targets, whether in relation to employment and wealth accumulation or in other spheres such as sport? Here, juggling with the race demographics of sports teams has replaced any focus on the genuine development of sporting capacity – and its prerequisite, equal access to good sports facilities – in all South African communities, from the youngest age. It is in this sphere that the tensions between merit-based selection, in the interest of national sporting pride and prestige, and race-based selection, in the interest of redressing demographic imbalances, are most blatantly evident to the public at large, and where media debates about team composition and pronouncements by politicians reinforce race thinking daily in the living rooms of all sports-loving South Africans.

Earlier, I quoted Mamphela Ramphele on affirmative action and the place of white women, where she drew attention to intra-race gender discrepancies. Her other point, about appointing people with skills inadequate to the demands of the jobs, has been confirmed many times, often from within the ANC and the government. Here municipal managers, and the disturbing numbers of failed towns, are singled out for attention annually. For example, in 2009 only seven of 278 municipalities in the whole of South Africa gained clean audit reports by the auditor-general ('an improvement on the previous year').[58] In 2010/2011 thirteen were given clean audits. Ratings Afrika reported that 'one of the major reasons remains the level of financial management and expertise, which are lacking or inadequate to apply the necessary financial discipline and principles'.[59] Early in 2014 the auditor-general informed parliament that 'most senior [government-employed] finance managers were failing to meet required competency standards, including at the level of chief financial officer'.[60] The parliamentary Standing Committee on Public Accounts called for a 'skills audit' in the finance and audit divisions of all government departments. But failure to 'meet competency standards' also calls for attention to be paid to the long-term process, starting at preschool, to ensure that the basic skills of participation in society, and of work, are made available to all. Prevalent 'unfair discrimination', such as exists in primary and secondary education or against girl children, leaves the later 'fair discrimination', when appointments are made in terms of the EEA, an empty promise for the majority. Emergency measures need to be taken, involving all citizens, whose skills can contribute to a more equal and humane society, wherever these skills may be found, with a willingness to employ them for the betterment of society.

The consequences of appointing unqualified people to jobs are multiple: the psychological damage to individual self-worth of those who fail and are blamed for their failure, and the effect on colleagues; the confirmation of racial stereotypes, both from outside and within the groups; and the resulting failures in service delivery for exactly the poor and marginalised whom the government aims to help.

This chapter has sketched both the unquestioned availability of racialism for decision-making in the post-1994 period, and the justification for its practical continuity in sense-making in policy formulation and law, and in the consequent practical demands of race-based criteria for measuring the success or failure of race-based steps towards social equality. However, it leaves a very important question: if apartheid had its census takers, race classification appeals board, Population Registration Act, identification documents and register, how does post-1994 classification work – how are the templates created and the vacant spaces filled in?

4

Classification without a law

POST-APARTHEID RACE CLASSIFICATION: HOW?

In 1991, the despised Population Registration Act of 1950 was abolished. It had already been amended in 1986, from which date new identity documents were to be issued that did not specify the holder's race. The amendment Act and its abolition five years later were events filled with irony when seen in retrospect, both because of the speakers who announced these changes (an apartheid minister, before the official end of apartheid, and then later the last apartheid president) and because of reactions to them. In 1986 Stoffel Botha, minister of home affairs, spoke in a debate in parliament about proposed amendments to the Act, through a new Identification Act. This was being introduced, he said, 'to do away with unnecessary passes and to replace them with a document that would be easy to carry and which would enable the police to perform their duties more easily … [A] strongly-bound reference book would be issued to all Africans (men and women) who had attained the age of 16.'[1] (The duties of the police were, of course, to enforce the hated 'pass laws' that controlled the movement of all black people and ensured the migrant labour and bantustan systems.) Botha said that the intention was to 'de-racialise' the identity documents issued to all South Africans: 'This new identity document which has been debated here is merely an instrument for identifying a person. It says *who* he is, and not *what* he is.'[2] The new Act 'introduced a single population register for all races' and a single document.[3] However, it did not do away with race classification, but included all on a general population register based on birth certificates, which required the identification of people's race.[4]

In effect, Botha acknowledged that he was returning – no matter in what small a measure – the faces of 'persons' ('who he is') to 'effaced specimens' ('what he is') of the very race categories in terms of which the government had legislated people's lives for the preceding four decades. This effacement had brought immense misery and degradation to millions. It had also damaged 'his own people' and all those South Africans who benefited from such dehumanisation of their fellow citizens. Not that it ended even the practice of classification – and apartheid in essence was to continue for another four years – but in the words used for the changes, it was a small step.

The Population Registration Act was finally abolished in full in June 1991, along with many other pieces of apartheid legislation. It was described, in parliament, as 'the mother of all apartheid laws', the 'cornerstone of apartheid', when the last apartheid-era president, F.W. de Klerk, signed the repealing legislation: 'The Population Registration Repeal Act made provision for people born after 27 June 1991 ... to no longer be classified in terms of race. However, past race classifications would be retained on the population register (which had been in existence since 1950).'[5] The retention of the population register (reflecting the already existing race entries) was justified by De Klerk because a 'race-based' governmental system was still in place at the time, in the form of a tricameral parliament of separate white, Coloured and Indian chambers. (In fact, it remained in place until the first democratic elections on 27 April 1994.) In a further irony, the Institute of Race Relations reported at the time: 'Critics of the government pointed out that the Population Registration Repeal Act provided for the abolition of race classification only for South Africans born after its enactment. People already classified in the population register on the basis of race would remain racially classified until the present racially based constitution was replaced by a non-racial constitution.'[6]

However, on the registration of births form that is still in use in the second decade of the twenty-first century, a section headed 'for medical and health use only' requires that the 'race' of the parents be given. Race classification of this type continues after death as well, as a cremation permission form for the eThekwini metro area, in which Durban is located, indicates.[7] This document includes the question: 'The race of the deceased was —'.

How does race classification work – for example, when 'fair discrimination' is required as part of a public or private sector search for candidates to fill a vacant position – now that the Population

Registration Act has been repealed? As I have argued in earlier chapters, there are two distinct, although inextricably interrelated, ways in which race classification takes place today, as it did under apartheid. First, and most important, is the level at which the state requires every single citizen, albeit in different ways and with different consequences, to accept being classified and at times to self-classify. Here, a central role in repeating the performance of race categorisation is played by legislation, the debates around policy, the definition of society that emerges through political discourse and mobilisation of constituencies, the classification of the population through the census, and the repeated requirement to complete forms when applying for any public service. The operation of this bureaucratic system (the conceptualisation and creation of templates for society) will be my focus in the first part of this chapter. Later, I will focus on the second level at which race classification occurs, that is, the more 'informal' dimensions of race thinking that are all-pervasive in the world in which we live and interact, in which we perceive people as individuals or as representatives of groups, and where the most profound consequences of race classification are felt in our personal and social lives. This world is very difficult to alter – there have to be reasons that are accepted by those participating, and it has to be accepted as a process and not an event.

These two levels of race classification both depend on an initial allocation to a race category, in distinct but articulating ways. The state-led, bureaucratic initial allocation, because it no longer is as openly and repugnantly formalised as under apartheid, occurs in fairly haphazard ways, as will be seen. There are bureaucratic processes demanded because of policy, but these are not coordinated and there are hardly ever stipulated guidelines for the classification of individuals into categories. And there is, at the second level, the social complicity of nearly all citizens in the formal process of allocation, because of the pervasiveness of previous practices of separation in accepting race belonging as common sense. To a large extent, we confirm the templates, the many forms and their four category boxes, into which we are placed on a regular basis. There may be no longer any official allocation through a Population Registration Act, but there is, and has been from 1994, official demand for race allocation.

After the naming of races and other designated groups in laws such as the Employment Equity Act and the Broad-Based Black Economic

Empowerment Act, the process of allocating individuals to race categories becomes (deliberately?) fuzzy. No one wants to use the term 'race classification' in what they do, and the term 'race' is avoided at times by the use of synonyms – ethnic group, cultural group, population group are the most common. These synonyms can cause confusion if they are taken literally, but then there will be someone to direct one to 'race'. No one wants to define what each of the four races is, and how they are to be recognised, at least not in the way that classification is practised in many thousands of sites all over the country. At these sites, it is left to the commonsense knowledge of lower-level bureaucrats. And no one wants to set the standards by which judgements are to be made to accompany any act of classification. Such measures would resemble far too closely the infamous apartheid 'pencil test' or its variations. So the names and the methods remain hidden, locked into the race thinking of those engaging in classification.

And here lies the rub. We all participate in keeping this system of classification operational, we are all expected to be its minions, because we can draw on the 'standards', implied in any classification, already familiar to us – in this case, the very criteria set by apartheid. This crude continuity need not be made explicit – in fact it cannot be, certainly not in the legislation of a fictive 'non-racial country'. But the state can rely on the fact that apartheid race thinking is still a firmly fixed classificatory grid in our minds. And we are expected not only to affirm this set of race categories through our willing collaboration in the classification process, but to teach the next generation, the 'born-frees', what those standards are. How else will they know whether they belong to a 'designated' or 'previously disadvantaged' group?

Without compulsory race classification we all become classifiers, simply by not questioning the existence of these categories. What Deborah Posel noted as the case under apartheid seems to apply even more in post-1994 South Africa: 'The Population Registration Act officially established race as a domain of knowledge independent of any particular training or experience, based instead on the ordinary experience of racial difference.'[8]

From the early 2000s the EEA was implemented with great fanfare, and was accompanied by threats, from labour lawyers and the state, of dire consequences if not immediately acted upon by employers. As Ivan Israelstam noted on a labour law website, 'those thousands of employers who do fall under the yoke of this legislation cannot afford not to comply with it. This is because the penalties for non-compliance are extremely harsh and include a maximum fine of R500 000.'⁹ The fines for non-compliance are potentially crippling and were employed as the stick. The then University of Natal, like all other academic institutions, was also required to adhere to the stipulations of this Act. When I raised the question with the university management of who was going to classify all of us into races, and how this would be done given that there was no definition of races in the Act, the response I received was a depressing and at times hostile one. The university had already appointed a 'specialist' with the specific job description of 'equity manager' and with responsibility for implementing the EEA. The correspondence between me and the university on this matter makes for fascinating reading as a small glimpse into how the new system was being created. Don't disturb; non-compliance would bring massive fines; you have all – as staff – already classified yourselves, so your race is lodged in your HR files, etc. An apology came later, but my questions about classification were not answered at the time. I was also told by the university's employment equity officer that 'We are not attempting a definition of "race". We do not have an "other" classification.' In the same year, 2000, all staff members were asked to 'verify' their personal details 'for tax and statutory purposes' – I was listed as 'Ethnic Group: White'.

Are we a society that is 'post-apartheid' or simply 'post-1994'? Is there a deliberate and imaginative examination of factors that maintain exclusion? Are we building a democracy based on our common human rights and shared values and aspirations as affirmed by the Constitution, or are we caught up in a process of improving – or destroying – 'race relations', the relationship between race groups? Are we playing with the fire that race classification keeps alive – the continued existence of groups who are expected to accept their race belonging, and yet not act on this when called upon to do so? Have we learnt the lessons of the 'minorities' created in societies that apply various systems of classification? And how do we deal with the use of race to mobilise and achieve certain sectional aims? What awful dangers are being incubated in the continuing maintenance and re-creation of 'minorities'? Some of those dangers have already been alluded to in this book, and many are all too visible if we look.

DERACIALISATION THROUGH RACIALISATION

The BBBEE Act of 2003 fitted into what Jimmy Manyi subsequently described as the process to 'deracialise the economy', ensuring that 'previously disadvantaged people [would] play a pivotal role in the mainstream economy'.[10] This was not a new idea at all, but had already featured in an address in 1983 by Chris Saunders, then chairman of the Tongaat Hulett Group, which was distributed as a booklet under the title *The future of Natal/KwaZulu: The pursuit of non-racial capitalism.*[11] It is filled with arguments that are fascinating to read in the context of BEE and other measures, and was initiated during a much-reviled moment of prefiguring attempts at reform in the province of Natal and the KwaZulu bantustan.[12] Let me give some examples of his arguments:

> I am assuming that no-one in this audience wishes anything but a free enterprise capitalist society for Natal/KwaZulu? I also assume that I do not have to convince anyone in the audience of the virtues of this ideology as opposed to that of Marxism. Perhaps, however, it is important for me to make the statement that capitalism does not necessarily cause racism as orthodox Marxism would assert. Neither does capitalism need racism in order to survive and prosper.[13]

Interestingly enough, Saunders quoted Neville Alexander as saying 'flatly, "A non-racial capitalism is impossible in South Africa." I don't subscribe to this point of view,' Saunders noted.[14] However, he did admit that capitalism was in a crisis as far as credibility went:

> One cannot escape the conclusion that deracialised, small-scale capitalism is always likely to be dominated by the wealth already created by racial monopoly capitalism no matter how hard the State may try to encourage small business ventures. This is a serious and worrying perception because if the Blacks are unable to join the entrenched monopolies, then only their break-up and socialisation will be seen as restoring justice and eliminating the crisis of credibility. It goes without saying, therefore, that a racial monopoly capitalism engenders racist socialism.[15]

Twenty years later, we have the BBBEE and some very successful 'generically black' participants in monopoly capitalism.

To return to Manyi: by 'mainstream economy' he means capitalist ownership and management (the very 'racial monopoly capitalism' to which Saunders referred), the field in which he operates, rather than the dirty field of production, where the overwhelming majority of black people have always been employed at the lowest levels of the job hierarchy. Manyi did not mention a letter from the ANC MP Ben Turok, written when the BBBEE Act was passed, in which he strongly criticised what went along with such policies: 'There are no instructions for them [ANC cadres] to conform to this lifestyle [a lifestyle appropriate to the status of the white elite]. The only political encouragement comes from the ANC policy of "deracialising the economy" and "black economic empowerment". In some cases this easily translates into practices of conspicuous consumption and greed despite the warnings from the ANC leadership.'[16] Four years earlier, President Thabo Mbeki had told a conference of the Black Management Forum: 'As part of the realisation of the aim to eradicate racism in our country, we must strive to create and strengthen a black capitalist class ... we have not made much progress and may very well be marching backwards with regard to the objective of deracialisation of ownership of productive property.'[17]

Hein Marais has defined two phases in BEE practice:

> the first, commenced in 1993 ... South African corporations masterminded and initiated the initial deals in the absence of an overarching framework ... By engineering these early BEE ventures, corporations in effect were managing their side of a tacit political compromise. The BEE deals would help lever the rapid emergence of a black African bourgeoisie sympathetic to the ideals of national liberation ... The thinking sat in a well-worn tradition that reserved a starring role for a patriotic bourgeoisie.[18]

However, 'there was strong disapproval and much moral condemnation of the narrow, elitist nature of BEE'. This meant that 'an overhaul was needed', and a Black Economic Empowerment Commission called for 'a more interventionist strategy', towards a wider (broad-based) approach attending to ownership, as well as 'affirmative action at senior management level, human resource development and employment equity'.[19] Marais comments that 'this more thoroughgoing variant of BEE, it was hoped, would cultivate a productive black capitalist elite capable of operating in tandem with government'.[20]

As with affirmative action or redress or employment equity, changing the face of ownership of capital has been slow. It has been extremely difficult to turn the policy of broad-based black economic empowerment into a reality for a significant number of people classified as black. The results of the implementation of the Act have been uneven and inequality has increased, especially within the generic black race groups.[21] Wealth at the top is increasing, along with the astonishingly conspicuous consumption to which Turok referred in his letter. BEE has certainly not been effective in altering the nature of capitalism, as was implied when the deracialisation of capitalism became a stated goal of post-1994 South Africa. In 2011 Jeremy Cronin, deputy minister of transport and deputy general secretary of the Communist Party, asked a 'simple question: does capital and, more specifically, does monopoly capital have a colour?' He continued, referring to ideas that were being contested in internal ANC debates at the time: 'When the "new tendency" and its demagogic vanguard rail against "white monopoly capital" what they are hearing is "white" and what they are thinking is "it's our turn now".'[22]

What black economic empowerment – and its legislated version in the BBBEE Act – has done is to reinforce the values of global consumer society, largely through the individuals who have benefited (no matter for how brief and precarious a time) and who have nearly all become conspicuous consumers in every visible aspect of their lifestyles. But most importantly, it has created a class, and aspiring members of that class, who link their futures to the unquestioned acceptance of race categories as well as of capitalism, based on the argument that, as apartheid was a racist and hence immoral system, there is moral justification for wealth acquisition by members of the races discriminated against, even if this involves the ethical somersault of benefiting from an exploitative system.

As I have indicated, the government's overall BEE strategy includes 'affirmative procurement practices' to ensure that businesses which apply for government tenders must meet the BEE requirements for quotas of different race groups employed, so that wealth gets transferred to individuals from formerly disadvantaged groups. This means that every application, whether for road or housing contracts, for the supply of stationery or for research projects, has to be vetted to see if the tenderer meets the racialised requirements. This, in turn, has led to the use of 'fronting', by appointing individuals as directors or co-owners who have no relevant qualifications or experience but are classified 'black', to ensure that the company has the correct quota of black management to be eligible for a tender – a practice severely criticised by the government.[23] It appears, though, from court cases that this does not mean that a black entrepreneur cannot win a tender bid for a contract and a healthy slice of the reward, and then employ a 'white company' to execute the task, because qualifying on the basis of being 'previously disadvantaged' does not guarantee that the winner will be capable of carrying out the work required. Already in 2002, soon after this policy was introduced, Stella Sigcau, the minister of public works, said that it 'had become apparent that some of the black contractors were under-quoting when tendering and had budgets that would not allow them to build good roads. Others put profits before quality.'[24] She drew attention to another problem, namely that 'black contractors', because of lack of equipment and material, were reliant on 'white-owned companies' to provide the services they were selling to the government, and were often being overcharged by the subcontractors. That is capitalism for you!

Such racial gate-keeping means that some person, some local, provincial or national government employee, has to make gate-keeping classificatory calls – but on the basis of what? Companies that re-engineer their staff quotas so that they are eligible for BEE contracts are doing so not necessarily because they support the goal of wealth redistribution, but because they see the profitable business sense in getting a good 'BEE scorecard'. BEE, as with other forms of affirmative action, relies not only on a veritable army of race classifiers and verifiers, but also on those serving as accredited BEE consultants. Under a heading 'Planned BEE reforms need scrutiny', Brigitte Brun, then 'Chief Operating Officer National Empowerment Rating Agency (KZN)' and now a 'B-BBEE verification specialist, and the chief operating officer of the AQRate rating agency', writes: 'Many black-owned companies are surprised that they are also expected to prove their BEE status emphasising their black ownership as proof of BEE compliancy – a process of public education needs to take place to communicate the requirements of the BEE Codes of Good Practice to all businesses.'[25]And in a 2007 newspaper supplement headed 'Battle of the BEEn counters', it was noted that 'what has never been tried before is the institutionalisation of an entire parallel accounting system such as the BEE Codes'.[26] The paper asked how it should be done: internally to the companies or through a process of external auditing? A month before, Colleen Wilson of the KwaZulu-Natal BEE Forum had provided an inventory of 'What business needs from BEE scorecard verification agencies'.[27] Auditing won out.

CENSUS AND THE DEMOGRAPHICS OF RACE

No discussion of the state and demographic classification can be complete without reference to the national census, which is central to race data collection.[28] Census-taking is a centralised process organised by Statistics South Africa, with literally millions of sites of classificatory practices: every household is required to complete the census form, often with the help of a 'census enumerator' who ensures that respondents give an answer, even if not always the 'correct' answer, to questions on the form. At these sites, a person responds to categories already chosen and justified on social scientific grounds as meaningful measures of national socio-economic characteristics, such as identity, education level, employment situation and material conditions of daily life. This is the core process through which the state decides – and it should never be forgotten that these are decisions, not just descriptions of what is supposedly already there, waiting to be recorded – what it wants to know about its citizens. Census bureaus, as Melissa Nobles puts it, are 'not politically neutral institutions, employing impartial methods, but state agencies that use census methods and data as instruments of governance'.[29] Nobles also cautions that 'counting by race is hardly a transparent process, because of the very conceptual ambiguities that surround race itself and the political stakes attached to it'.[30] It both reflects and creates official versions of social reality (existing or intended) and, therefore, the need for information about this (socially constructed) reality – hereby reinforcing the versions required by the questions.

From the time of the first census, the social categories used in census exercises in southern Africa have always indicated some form of shifting distinction between group identities, reflecting ideas imported from elsewhere about the races in the country. We have seen how the apartheid state used the first census controlled by the National Party in 1951 to give content to the Population Registration Act, and hence to the race- and language-based ethnic separations of apartheid policy.[31] The ANC, too, conducted a census soon after taking power in 1994, with the essential goal of enumerating and classifying all South Africans, now acknowledged to be citizens in an inclusive state. This first census, undertaken in 1996, seemed to offer an opportunity to imagine a world beyond the one South Africans were leaving behind. However, race was much more systematically embedded in the operation of the state than simply in the imagination of its citizens. The first post-1994 census, like all subsequent ones, continued to rely on the paradigm underlying the Population Registration Act, employing apartheid race categories along with socio-economic measures to classify individuals and households. Mark Orkin, eminent sociologist and statistician-general at the time, commented in another context – the use of race categories in medical research – as follows: 'It is a *non sequitur* to argue from the abuse of the population group variable by some analysts that it should in general be excluded from cogent analysis. Apartheid perverted lots of concepts; we need to reclaim them rather than abandon them.'[32] Here is a powerfully located social scientist calling races 'population groups', as apartheid had done (to avoid having to use the term 'race'), turning it simply into a 'concept' and asking for it to be rehabilitated by social science.

Melissa Nobles has traced changes in race and ethnic categories in Brazil and the US through the history of census-taking from the first census in each country up to 2000. She was concerned to find out what the motivation was for employing certain categorisations, and what the reasons were for changing them, as they never stay exactly the same. She came to the conclusion that census categories, as with all classifications of human beings, create rather than describe what is to be found. The variations she found in categories provided clear evidence of the effective creation, rather than reflection, of categories of citizens in Brazil and the US.[33] Kertzer and Arel argue similarly: 'the census does much more than simply reflect social reality; rather it plays a key role in the construction of that reality. In no sector is this more importantly the case than in the ways in which the census is used to divide the national population into separate identity categories: racial, ethnic, linguistic, or religious.'[34]

But what if the categories had already been created, providing the 'prior vocabulary' to the identification of 'facts'?[35] In the South African census, one of the crudest acknowledgements of the continuity of apartheid race categories is the case of the 'born-frees', those who were born after 27 April 1994 – how are these individuals to be assigned to a race category? Here, it cannot be 'as you were classified under apartheid'. In instructions given to census enumerators for the 2004 census, they 'were advised that a population group was: "A group with common characteristics (in terms of descent and history), particularly in relation to how they were (*or would have been*) classified before the 1994 elections." … In this manner those born since 1994 were brought within the ambit of apartheid race classification!'[36]

Thus, it is these cohorts of enumerators who have continued to implement a government policy to classify South Africans racially – even as recently as the 2011 census, seventeen years after the establishment of a 'non-racial democracy'. And the practice continues to be justified in the same terms that were used in 1996. In a brief exchange I had in 2005 with the statistician-general and head of Statistics South Africa, Pali Lehohla, he argued that 'some identifier of population group [*sic*] is, at least for a time, probably required to measure and monitor progress in redressing the inequalities of South Africa's past'.[37]

OTHER SITES AND PRACTICES: CLASSIFICATION BY NOBODY[38]

It is at the lower levels of officialdom that the full extent of active involvement by thousands upon thousands of people in the system of race classification becomes visible. Formally, there are no longer race classification documents issued by the state as there were under apartheid, but in fact these documents are created and exist in the personnel records of every company that employs people, every education institution that receives state funding, every police station that records an accident, every hospital where a baby is born – and in many other contexts where individuals engage with organisations that keep records about them. As Shaun Ruggunan and I have written in a report on the findings of a research study into classification:

> generally classification processes [in post-1994 South Africa] are undertaken by individuals at lower levels in the organisational hierarchy to whom responsibility for doing so has been devolved, often as a default requirement rather than as a formal job description. These individuals may have differing interpretations of policy requirements and may attach different weight to the implications of the processes and practices of classification itself.[39]

Functionaries engaged in such classificatory processes easily identify the reasons for doing so as 'legislative requirements' or 'the policy of the organisation', flowing from the legislation. Policy implementation of this type can be devolved to lower levels within organisations where 'equity plans' have to be drawn up and then approved by higher authority – these plans rest on quantification of races, and also sex and disability. In the case of some institutions, for example the University of KwaZulu-Natal, the results of this counting exercise then appear on the institution's website, or are used in advertisements to show its commitment to 'transformation'. 'Increasingly there is no space in South African work organisations not to be racially classified ... Where employees refuse to self-classify or challenge classification they are assigned a classification by human resources. Every column in the required reports has to be completed with the options already designated.'[40]

The claim that we, as South African citizens, spontaneously and willingly 'self-classify' is often used by people who monitor the completion of forms, collect data and create tables. It is the response given by Statistics South Africa when asked to comment on race classification in the census data-gathering process. This approach serves two purposes: making everyone complicit in the classification process and thereby avoiding taking responsibility for being classifiers. In the case of UKZN (and, by implication, in all reporting institutions), the Ruggunan and Maré study found that because tables had to be completed – as legislatively required, for reporting purposes, or to be able to make claims of success in the business of race equity – adjustments were always made to the category choices of individual respondents by the responsible bureaucrats within the institution if they disagreed with the respondents' choices, and blocks were subsequently ticked where the respondents had not done so:

> When prompted as to how individuals can err in self-classification, respondents [engaged in the process] argued that it was often an attempt to secure access to financial resources or a deliberate attempt by academic staff to hinder transformation processes. Therefore, for example, it can be argued to be a 'moral' error in the eyes of the bureaucrat: race classification has consequences, so the self-classifier has to accept not only the classification as common-sense, but also the consequences, whether favourable or not.

However, bureaucrats deem that *self*-classification can also be *inaccurate* against 'objective' criteria, rather than just 'cheating'. They argue that they are objective observers who can recognise the phenotypic and other markers, such as surnames, place of residence and schooling, aspects that may challenge the race that individuals have classified themselves as – races are facts and confirmed by other facts.[41]

Thus, because of the cascading pressures within organisations, the government can now argue that the public is prepared to comply and acknowledge race as an obvious, everyday aspect of what it means to be a South African, and thereby submit to a political vision for which, it seems, there is truly no imaginable or desirable alternative in official thinking.

Of course, this classification does not always happen without a certain amount of agonising on the part of those responsible. In 2007, for example, a teacher in the Eastern Cape town of Graaff-Reinet appealed to the Department of Education for help after she had enquired about the 'race' of a child in her class (as required for effective completion of a departmental monitoring form), and was told by the child, 'Miss, I'm mixed, so just call me black.' According to a newspaper report, the teacher 'wondered if the department could provide guidelines on how to go about classification. "How black is black? And when is a pupil a coloured?"' The same report referred to 'a teacher at Uitenhage [who] says if she can't tell the race of pupils from their skin colour, she looks at their surnames – "failing that, I ask the pupil".'[42]

On rare occasions the difficulties of dealing with the classification question lead to court proceedings – as we saw with the Chinese Association challenge. Another case that deserves mention confronted the question of how to deal with demographically restricted bequests, specifically those willed to fund education for young people, where the beneficiaries-to-be are described in race (or sex) terms. In the case heard in the Cape High Court in December 2011, Judge Patricia Goliath focused her attention on the issue of race classification, and not just on the discriminatory nature of such bequests. The case was brought by the Board of Executors (BoE), which administered three trusts specifying that bursary allocations might be made only to students who were variously 'Europeans', 'members of the White Group', 'members of the white population group', 'of British descent' and male. The BoE provided support for their case, seeking to remove these restrictions, by calling two expert witnesses. The first was Dr Colleen O'Ryan, a geneticist, who 'concluded that race is scientifically not a meaningful concept and that it is not possible on any scientific grounds to differentiate any two individuals into distinct race subspecies'. The second was Dr Hans Heese, a social historian, who 'emphasized the arbitrariness inherent in seeking to classify individuals into racial groups. He concluded that no reasonable genealogist would endeavour to classify individuals into specific groups based on race.'[43] On the basis of the evidence the BoE conceded that 'these provisions are offensive, arbitrary and a concept that is undefined and meaningless'. The argument was further made that the references were 'to race classification of South Africans into racial groups pursuant to the provisions of the now repealed Population Registration Act 30 of 1950. Hence, there currently exists no white group in South Africa.' Judge Goliath supported the BoE's application, on the grounds of unfair discrimination and previous cases, but unfortunately did not seem to refer to the expert witnesses and their arguments in her judgment. She, therefore, did not address the basis for race classification.

Post-1994 race classification is, in effect, 'classification by nobody', because no one needs to take responsibility for the act of classification of each individual – neither the lower-level bureaucrats at a university, nor the police agent in the charge office, nor the human resources officer in all employing institutions, nor the teachers in all schools, despite the fact that they effectively create and fix race identities for the people they deal with. These are fellow human beings having to ask the questions, correct the 'self-classifications', complete the forms, submit the information. What effect does this task have on at least some of them, those who remember the past humiliation of having to carry a pass, those who see race classification as demeaning, as counter to the foundational value of human dignity on which the Constitution rests?

CLASSIFICATION WITHOUT THE NEED FOR LAWS

In their book *Sorting Things Out*, Bowker and Star point to the way in which classification 'naturalised' itself in apartheid South Africa, and continues to do so post-1994:

> As layers of a classification system become enfolded into a working
> infrastructure, the original political intervention becomes more and more

firmly entrenched. In many cases, this leads to a naturalisation of the political category, through a process of convergence. It becomes taken for granted. (We are using the word naturalisation advisedly here, since it is only through our infrastructures that we can describe and manipulate nature.) We emphasise here the stubborn refusal of 'race' to fit the desired classification system suborned by its pro-apartheid designers.[44]

The distress felt by the Eastern Cape teachers (no doubt among many others in a similar position) at their inability to classify without guidance or legal definition, without 'standards', is a reflection of one of the central questions asked by Bowker and Star: 'What happens to the cases that do not fit?'[45]

The answer is that there are no cases that do not fit. All South Africans lived under apartheid and were race-classified by that system. And if one person belongs to a race, all others do so as well. There is no situation where 'we belong to a race, but the rest of you do not', or 'you belong to a race but I do not'. But there are situations where contortions of sense-making have to be employed to hold onto notions of race categories – when we make exceptions to our ideas of race. Bureaucracies cannot allow exceptions, but everyday life experiences demand exceptions of us.

Through race classification under apartheid, every individual benefited or was deprived of benefits. New arrivals, such as those born after 1994, have inherited the consequences of previous benefits or the effects of previous discrimination and, therefore, belong to the races of the past – so the argument implicitly goes. Nor can race be escaped or rejected, for it is defined as an essential aspect of every individual – it overrides the material effects of advantage or of discrimination. If you were poor, then and now, this does not remove you from being 'white'; if you were rich, then and now, this does not cancel out your 'generic blackness'.

At least, this is what the ruling party's political vision of a race-based society would have us believe, and this is what its laws and moral exhortations, its calls on 'victors' and 'the guilty', push us towards integrating into our daily lives. And yes, as I have argued, the common sense of race prevails, overwhelmingly, in South Africa. But there is not just one such way of thinking about this question – as witness the court challenges, the critical opinion pieces, the uneasy compromises made by former liberation struggle activists with the new political hegemony. For an increasing number of South Africans, race is indeed a manifestly social construct and, therefore, can be socially deconstructed and replaced with more meaningful categories of social difference, categories more useful to working towards an equal society based on dignity. Therein lies the challenge: against enormous odds, and the might of state classificatory practices and thinking, to rethink the framework for answering the question who we are as South Africans and as human beings, how we are different, how we are diverse, and how we are the same; to rethink our histories in their local and global entanglement. From the moment this question is raised in individual thinking, the banality of daily race thinking will be challenged, individually or collectively.

Patterns of race categorisation rest on the 'naturalization of the political category' about which Bowker and Star write. As they argue about classification in general, 'these standards and classifications, however imbricated in our lives, are ordinarily invisible'.[46] They will remain so unless the people directly affected by such classification – and that means all South Africans – challenge its existence and its power over their lives, as part of a broader struggle against the power relations embedded in race thinking, in class exploitation and gender domination. It was in that confrontation with power – including the power of ideology – that the commitment to a 'non-racial' future lay during the decades of struggle against apartheid. And it was as part of this struggle that Biko's Black Consciousness philosophy was formulated as a direct challenge to apartheid, putting forward instead a vision of a shared 'blackness', a shared identity and a shared humanity. This vision, moreover, was concretised in creative community initiatives as well as in acts of resistance that refused to limit themselves to the concern of any racially defined subset of the oppressed. It is an irony, but not so surprising, that under an ANC government an exactly inverse deconstruction of 'blackness' should be occurring, such that groups of formerly oppressed individuals are now pitted against each other in a competition for access to 'a better life for all' and to the wealth of the country.

CONSEQUENCES AND REACTIONS

Race classification has consequences. Confirmation of the existence of separate race groups leads, obviously, to behaviour patterns, claims and antagonisms based on such classification. By way of concluding my analysis of post-1994 race thinking in South Africa, I will briefly discuss here a few of the most immediate consequences that flow directly from, or remain unexamined because of, the commonsense acceptance of race categories in all spheres of social and political life.

If the present government's justification for retaining race-based policies is taken into account, then an essential objection to it is that the effects of these policies not only fail in moving this society towards one more equal than it was under apartheid, but contribute towards creating a society which is becoming more unequal than it ever has been. Previously, the correlation of inequality with races was there for all to see – the exceptions were few. Now, and increasingly, inequality within the races is growing fastest. For inequality as a central feature of society relates not only to the outcomes of various contested economic models, but also to the mindsets that separate poverty from wealth and deny any causal link between them, in effect preventing any examination of the root cause of such a state. It relates to the physical separation of the wealthy from the poor; to the totally self-centred and insensitive displays of consumption, sugar-coated with equally vulgar displays of 'charity' towards 'the poor'; and, finally, to the protection that the state provides to a capitalist system that, under any social circumstances, reproduces structural inequality.

The statement uttered by an ANC politician in the 1990s, that he did not 'struggle' to be poor, is the iconic slogan of the present. It does not include the argument that 'we did not struggle to live with poverty'. The effect of BEE policies, whether broadly or narrowly defined, has been to sanctify the struggles of black individuals to become 'filthy rich' (to use Phumzile Mlambo-Ngcuka's accurate term) without asking them to take notice of the millions of other equally 'formerly disadvantaged' citizens who have not been liberated from their impoverished situations.[47] The argument that BEE policies introduce a more socially responsible or 'patriotic' version of capitalism, based on the notion that black capitalists are more committed to *ubuntu* than their white counterparts, is given the lie by the growing wealth gap in South Africa. (Ironically, it also protects capitalists classified as white from full criticism, apart from their not doing enough to create black capitalists.) The hopelessness of this argument reveals itself in the tortured utterances of government ministers on the subject, such as the following by the minister of public enterprises, Malusi Gigaba, in 2013:

115

Exploring economic opportunities for the poor, advocating for access to capital at reasonable prices with less stringent conditions and developing investment products that are customised to the lifestyle of the working poor are some of the important initiatives black business and executives can undertake.

This would be a measure of their patriotism.

In the last eight months, workers in the mining sector and other industries have demanded economic justice and a stake in the economy.

The response of the mining sector was to threaten disinvestment citing high input cost and decline of global demand. This behaviour forced the ruling party and the government to remind the sector of the conducive environment created for it to grow.

The sector has flourished over the years on the back of cheap inputs provided by the government, ranging from cheap electricity, cheap labour cost, cheap rail and cargo cost and yet when workers demand a living wage and decent working conditions, the country is threatened with disinvestments.

Some black executives are part of these decisions and yet do not challenge the system, which would be a measure of their patriotism.[48]

The dream of a 'deracialisation of capitalism' that has inspired people like Jimmy Manyi to argue for spatial-racial corrective engineering will not ever produce the hoped-for end result. The goal of a demographically correct racialised utopia is a fiction, one that suits some present interests but not the country as a whole: it demands a degree of social engineering and fixing of race categories beyond anything achieved by apartheid. Instead of indulging in race-based fantasies of numerical proportional 'equality', the true achievement of this goal depends on seeking solutions to the real challenges facing *all* South Africans: finding decent work, providing proper education, eliminating poverty and inequality, and reversing the inevitable negative consequences of capitalist growth.

Probably the most urgent, and terrifying, of the consequences of race classification in post-1994 South Africa lies in the effect of creating easily identifiable categories of people and then employing negative descriptors or blame when referring to those groups. This is a recipe for disaster: racist behaviour on the part of one specimen of a category becomes seen as the racism of all, corruption of one necessarily becomes the corrupt tendencies of all within the category of which he or she is a specimen. This is especially the case when the woes of all in the majority race group, and the failure of the state, are blamed on identifiable minority groups; or, for that matter, when racist or racialist members of minorities find their stereotypes confirmed by the behaviour of any specimen of the majority group. The process works dialectically, with labelling from outside being confirmed by and feeding on group formation from within. Settlers from Europe provide an interesting case study of group formation, intermixing and fragmentation, through domination and in-group formation. One segment within that group was ultimately racialised into a single 'white' political unit, the Afrikaners, for whom an inaccurate purity was claimed. There are, at present, very few Afrikaners who would not see themselves as individual citizens of South Africa, albeit still racialised as a distinct race among other distinct races. Other minority groups whose formation was subject to similar processes, albeit with quite different content and histories, are Indians, Coloureds, and ethnic subgroups such as Shangaan and Zulu South Africans.

A clear example of the potential dangers of race-based categorisation relates to the category described as Indian. Mala Singh and Shahid Vawda raised a red flag in this regard even before the transition to democracy began, when they drew attention to the case of the Natal Indian Congress, where tensions had surfaced around whether to continue as a sectional organisation:

A serious attempt at addressing the material specificities of the Indian community would require taking into account the way in which differing material interests within the community intersect with interests defined in relation to the country as a whole across the racial divide. Within a struggle towards non-racialism, identifying a political constituency like 'Indian Community' is not as neutral a choice as choosing to organise among women or workers or students or health care workers.[49]

The concern voiced by Singh and Vawda was not without foundation. In 2002, the prominent musician and theatre personality Mbongeni Ngema gave threatening voice to the homogenisation of the category Indian when he wrote a song, *AmaNdiya* (the Indians), which circulated widely. The Zulu lyrics of the song included the lines 'Indians don't want to change, even Mandela has failed to convince them. It was better with whites, we knew then it was a racial conflict.'[50] With memories of the

'Indian–African' violence in Natal in 1949 still fresh,[51] the implications of Ngema's stereotyping were ominous. Subsequently, Fikile Mbalula, the ANC Youth League president, reminded this 'community' of their precarious location as 'outsiders':

> 'These days you are seeing the shrinking of actual numbers of African students and when you enter the institution [UKZN], you can actually think that you are in India or Mumbai, or whatever the case,' he said.
>
> This was borne out by the university's own commission of inquiry amid concerns as to why African students were dropping out in their first year, given issues of curriculum content and affordability, Mbalula said.
>
> Mbalula said on Monday that even with hindsight, the language he used could not be considered racist.
>
> 'It's a non-issue. It's just that it's blown out of context to peddle on racist undertones.'
>
> In reaction, ANC spokesperson Tiyani Rikhotso said: 'In raising the challenges of transformation of higher education, we hope Mbalula didn't mean to cause any discomfort to the Indian community'.[52]

In a contribution to the *Mail & Guardian*, Loren Landau, director of the African Centre for Migration and Society at the University of the Witwatersrand, warned that situations where peace seems to exist between 'locals' and 'foreigners', of whatever description, 'may not mean that the demons have been tamed'. He referred to a case where Indians were told to 'go home' by the mayor of a KwaZulu-Natal town, and added:

> In 2012, in a kind of inclusive chauvinism, rioters in Rustenburg threatened 'Indian' South African shopkeepers with violence and taunts, calling them *amakwerekwere*, a term previously reserved for foreigners of African origin. Around the country, people of Asian and Indian descent, including those who have lived here for generations [and who are South African citizens], confront such sentiments – as do foreigners from across the continent and beyond.[53]

In 2014 in KwaZulu-Natal there were three organised predominantly anti-Indian bodies: the Mazibuye African Forum (MAF), the Imbumba Business Empowerment Group (IBEG), and the political party

Ubumbano Lwesizwe Sabangoni (ULS). Receiving publicity greater than the others, the MAF, through member Phumlani Mfeka, said that the forum 'is a social movement that aims to address the question of African indigenous priority in South Africa, with the indigenous people being Africans and mixed race Africans, also termed coloured'.[54] Drawing on the precedent of compensation for Jews by Germany after World War II, and efforts by 'Asian countries [such as Malaysia and India] ... to reverse the effects of colonialism',[55] Mfeka advanced a list of steps that included 'ring-fenced procurement directed at African-founded, -owned and -controlled business', and the representation of Africans 'in at least their demographic proportions' in the public and private sectors. But, as before in the MAF's actions and statements, Indians were the real target: 'there is overwhelming evidence that Indians are over-represented in the private and public sectors of the South African economy ... Indians should henceforth be removed as needing affirmative action because they have exceeded their demographic targets of representation.' He added that 'Africans are a dispossessed indigenous people with little to no support from outside the continent. The Indian community on the other hand arrived in South Africa as immigrants and still has ties as well as political and cultural support from India.' (Arjun Appadurai's warning of the fear of small numbers is, unfortunately, totally apposite. He notes the 'anxiety of incompleteness', available to the majority to blame for failures of various kinds.)[56] The premier of the province, Senzo Mchunu, had already formed a 'task team' to investigate the MAF's accusations of unfair favouritism. Mchunu picked on some of the implications, especially for his party during an election year, and warned that 'Anything that smells of race and anything that threatens the life and limb of any community we are not going to tolerate'.[57] But in post-1994 South Africa everything 'smells of race' in the official template.

Similar threats involving South Africans who categorise themselves – or are categorised by the state – as Coloureds, Chinese or whatever have led, on the one hand, to court challenges, in which individuals argue for justice based on their membership of a race group. On the other hand, they have also led to the formation of defensive sectional interest groups such as the Chinese Association, the Bruin Belange-Inisiatief, the Bruin Bemagtigingsbeweging and, for their largely Afrikaans-speaking members and concerns, AfriForum and the trade union Solidarity. The dangers of this tendency are summed up by Neville Alexander: 'To define yourself into a minority corner in a situation such as the transition in South Africa is to play with fire in an almost literal sense. There is nothing more dangerous.'[58]

A PRELIMINARY CONCLUSION

The racial order firmly established by successive minority governments in South Africa over the course of the twentieth century was inherited by the first democratic government in 1994. This legacy consisted in part of what Colette Guillaumin refers to as notions of race embedded in the form of 'relationships regarded as racial by those directly and actually involved'.[59] The question I asked in Chapter 1 – 'why is the race classification legacy of apartheid *not* seen as an unwanted legacy of that despised system?' – is answered, I have argued, by the fact that most opponents of apartheid, and particularly members of the ANC, never properly questioned the race categories and the embedded race thinking that informed their own political vision and programme.

My argument in Part Two has been that race thinking, and the practices it gives rise to, have continued since 1994 with hardly a question being raised. The ANC government's strategy of using race-based policies to bring about an equal society and economic redress has been unsuccessful, and has criminally distracted us from exploring alternative and much more widely inclusive ways of tackling our problems. Instead, these policies have entrenched even further a racialised understanding of who we are as South Africans, and have blocked off other avenues for exploring ways to address the very real psychological trauma and social inequalities bequeathed by apartheid. Dissident voices have been sidelined, or attempts have been made to silence them. Certainly, no state-driven efforts have been made to open up critical debate on even such an admirable and oft-repeated notion as 'non-racialism', despite the constitutional commitment to this goal.

The use of race classification cannot ever be separated from its origin in efforts to separate and diminish the human worth of individuals; the ends to which race thinking is put (no matter how phrased) cannot be separated from a history of race-based discrimination and dehumanising oppression; the blame for ongoing reliance on race categories in government policy cannot be laid at the door of apartheid, not when race has been written into law (including the Constitution) and when race classification is demanded of every single citizen. The irony is that it should be a democratic South Africa, a society hailed across the world for having achieved victory over a racist regime, that is carrying race forward as an undisputed category into the twenty-first century. Race classification – as well as the retention, confirmation, reproduction and extension to new generations of race categories – is in itself, no matter the justification, a crime against humanity.

PART THREE

5

The imagined enemy
that serves a purpose

The transition from a nomadic life to a settled one is said to mark the beginning of what was later called civilization. Soon all of those who survived outside the city began to be considered uncivilized. But that is another story – to be told in the hills near the wolves.

– John Berger[1]

Why are the streets and squares emptying so quickly,
And everybody turning home again so full of thought?
Because night has fallen and the Barbarians have not come.
And some people have arrived from the frontier;
They said there are no Barbarians any more.

And now what will become of us without Barbarians? –
Those people were some sort of solution.

– CP Cavafy[2]

The Greek tragedians, when they had invented the barbarians, soon began to play with the 'inner barbarism' of Greeks. Perhaps part of the otherness of the barbarians was that, unlike the civilised, they were morally all of a piece – not dualistic characters in which good nature warred with bad, but whole ...

Barbarians were homogeneous; civilised people were multiform and differentiated.

– Neal Ascherson[3]

ALTERNATIVES TO RACE THINKING

There is no easy way out. The past rests heavily on the present, constraining the way in which we are able to think about the future. It can cramp the imagination; confirm what exists as though it is unchanging, primordial; shape our decisions about what is good and bad, desirable and undesirable. We are trapped, often, in the sedimentation of old ways of thinking, of experiences, imaginings of experiences, of tales told of the past and of ways in which we should make use of that past – trapped also in the ways we perceive those stories to be inviolable. Then preventing change, or at best controlling it, becomes desirable. We have to maintain the notion of a dangerous 'other', which explains our own actions – in Cavafy's poem, 'the barbarians' served that purpose, were 'some sort of solution'.

There are understandable, even if not very productive, ways of making sense of race in our lives in South Africa. Race can serve as an anchor for 'legitimate' anger at remaining 'legacies', a reason for their continuing existence; as a repository of memory in which reflection on the grief of apartheid can make sense; as a framework within which we 'understand' what 'they' did to 'us', or make sense of why 'they' continue to do this to 'us' (and here the 'us' and 'they' may well change or have changed); as a locus of social identity that provides existential security, a sense of belonging with those who are 'like me'; as a resource that serves us cynically as a mobilising fuel for political or material reasons or a justification for horrifying behaviour against specimens of the category of the other. The focus of my concern in the present work has been the deliberate demand for race classification by the ANC-controlled state since 1994. The state, however, avoids – in what can only be described as devious ways – any direct responsibility for these practices, or any accountability for the full range of their consequences. Those consequences are more than glimmers of the potential dangers after twenty years of an inclusive democracy.

I will say it again: classification of fellow humans into 'races', through the power granted to the state, remains a crime against humanity, no matter what justification is offered. The consequences are there to see. Kwame Appiah addresses such issues in the concluding section to his book *The Honor Code*: 'Finally, morality itself requires us to recognize that every human being has, other things being equal, a fundamental right to respect that we term *dignity*. Dignity is a form of honor, too, and *its* code is part of morality.'[4] Dignity, with all its implications of social justice, equality, safety, a life worth living, may be the bedrock of the South African Constitution, but it is contradicted in every one of the millions of instances of race classification – and by the very state that is meant to uphold and advance the constitutional commitment to ensuring dignity. Race classification does not allow for dignity, neither that of the classified nor that of the classifiers.

A commitment to action that corrects the wrongs of the past should be a continuation of the previous commitment to undermining apartheid. Such action, in both cases, is rooted in the commitment to the principle of dignity: the dignity of greater equality, and the dignity of achieving it in ways opposite to those that formed the basis of apartheid's deliberate inequality. This book is a call to all to be part of the process of finding solutions to those problems besetting contemporary South Africa.[5] The problems are real, whether as 'legacies' of the past (and there are enough of those, including race classification) or as failure in the present. That is the challenge in this, one of the most unequal and violent societies in the early twenty-first century. South Africa is not a war zone, but we have been described as being at war with ourselves. It is a war that pits the categories of people we have created against each other – class, sexuality, gender, citizenship, ethnicity and race. Race classification – and the race thinking which it confirms – not only stands in the way of finding solutions, but actually contributes in essential ways to the problems we need to solve.

I have placed myself, my personal experience, in this book, in order to indicate what individuals, born into and enclosed by group belonging, have to confront in order to escape the categories imposed on all; but also to make the case that escape is possible for anyone. Not that it is easy to achieve, but then neither is voicing dissenting opinions against those in power in any society. To quote Judith Butler, in words that speak for many, then and now: 'To continue to voice one's views under those conditions is not easy, since one must not only discount the truth of the appellation, but brave the stigma that seizes up from the public domain.'[6] Butler was writing about the post-9/11 context in the US, where the pressure to opt for simple answers to difficult questions about US relations with the world was very strong, and inquiring or critical voices were stigmatised as 'traitors' or 'terrorist sympathisers'. She asks,

'What can I do with the conditions that form me?'[7] As I have made clear, we are all formed by the world into which we are born, but we are each born with the capacity to reflect on and change ourselves and the world we live in. What is more, the past need not stifle initiative. After all, the end of apartheid indicated the success of a variety of forms of rejection of an existing political system, expressed and enacted by the overwhelming majority of South Africans. Even most of those who had benefited materially from apartheid voted against its continuation in 1992, for a variety of reasons.

Zygmunt Bauman, whom I have referred to often in these chapters, draws together several strands of what I present in this concluding section of my argument:

> I'd say that the twin roles which we, sociologists, are called on to perform in that dialogue [between common sense and critical thinking] are those of the *defamiliarizing the familiar* and *familiarizing* (taming, domesticating) *the unfamiliar* ... [These twin roles] call for skills in uncovering the 'doxa' (the knowledge we think with but not about), pulling it out of the murky depths of the subconscious, and so enabling and setting in motion a process of perpetual critical scrutiny, and perhaps even conscious control over its contents, by those who are thus far unaware of possessing it and of unwittingly using it. In other words, they call for the art of *dialogue*.[8]

So, in the first instance, Bauman issues the challenge to sociology, or to any critical thinking about contemporary society, to disturb what seems to be obvious and unchangeable, and come to grips with that which causes uncertainty and fear (the belief in 'barbarians at the gate'). These are conditions that – if left undisturbed – serve only the interests of the powerful in society.

In the second instance, Bauman acknowledges the power of 'doxa', of everyday thinking, and places it within the field of that which we need to think about and not just think with.[9] But we first have to become aware that we operate with the belief that we 'know it all', that our common sense provides us with understanding and security.

And, in the third instance, Baumann calls for dialogue, the free exchange of thought between people – and not interaction shaped by the assumption of an 'us and them' situation, by a lack of curiosity about fellow human beings, because they have been summed up by stereotyping, or fear, or hatred, by that 'prior vocabulary', the language of categorisation that already exists.

In this final section, I will bring my argument to a close. First, I will turn to the need for challenging and imaginative approaches to tackling the commonsense burden of the present (and hence of the past), expressed in the call for utopian thinking. This means deliberately creating a new vocabulary for a society which must still be brought into being, rather than working with that which we have inherited. Next, I will return to the issue of non-racialism, not as an event or an empty claim but as part of that world of challenging possibilities opened up through utopian thinking, the world which we must work towards and which we can already glimpse. Third, I will consider some approaches flowing from an acceptance of the challenge to create a South Africa more equal and more human (in the sense of morality and ethics, of dignity, of realising human capabilities) than the one we were bequeathed in 1994. This is where the way out has to be located, in creating a world beyond all three of these legacies: beyond race, beyond exploitation and inequality, and beyond notions of tradition that deny full humanity to many, especially women and children.

The possibility of change depends on the realisation that there are questions to be asked. That challenge is also captured in the dedication at the start of this book, expressed in the words of C Wright Mills's daughter to her father: 'I learned about the importance of simultaneously maintaining a healthy respect for complexity and a great capacity for outrage.'

DISTURBING THE FAMILIAR: BEYOND COMMON SENSE

Writing this book has been very difficult. Here I am thinking not only of the obvious issues of time and resources, but of recognising the absolute necessity of another social order, while simultaneously acknowledging the apparent impossibility of change happening when one confronts something as enormous as a racialised capitalist society. How to bring about change, when the majority in South Africa probably do not wish to relinquish race, when those in power depend on maintaining race thinking, when some of those challenging the existing powers see the opportunity to do so with the help of potentially catastrophic race (and national and ethnic) populism, and when challenges again focus on the purpose and consequences of classification to the exclusion of questioning the use of race? And yet, confronting race thinking is core to any project that is serious about changing South African society in fundamental ways. My conviction about this is rooted in my early experience 'from the inside', from the 'heart of darkness', of the dehumanisation of others that occurs from within the apparently secure enclaves of ethnically and racially defined groups. By 'apparent impossibility of change', I am referring to the extreme difficulty of bringing about change from within a social world that rejects the need for this aspect of transformation – a transformation that alters what seem to be essential characteristics of all things as they are, things necessary to our well-being and even survival.

This society from which I write seems incapable of changing the way in which it classifies and sees people. It is a society that seems so bound to what is (no matter how false and demeaning that picture may be) that it cannot imagine what could be or should be. Thousands and thousands of words are repeated daily, in every context of our lives, in the firm knowledge that all those who read and hear them know what they mean: black African, Coloured, Indian, white. Race is our cognitive lingua franca, the language we share, used to confirm what we are made to believe we don't share.

Moments of critical and open reflection are very difficult to imagine, and yet … Much the same was felt about the impossibility of ending apartheid, by many who wished it would change, but could not imagine how this might happen. But apartheid did end, in fundamental ways, because the majority of people refused to accept the state's forcibly imposed versions of the social world, of what exists and what is good. An attempt was made under apartheid to establish a dominant ideology rooted in race thinking, with each individual enclosed within a 'community of similarity', whose actions were then motivated by 'mixophobia'.[10] But the imposition of this ideology depended on increasingly repressive measures and in the end did not succeed, because the National Party's political vision was critically examined, experienced as false, and seen increasingly as a social construct that was open to change. This does not mean that all opposition, thankfully, accepted a single vision of the social world – young people took to the streets in 1976 in part because they felt their parents had failed; the Inkatha movement mobilised Zulus on an ethnic basis to oppose that apartheid grand scheme of 'independence', while others accepted ethnic politics fully; the Communist Party represented one version of class interests, while the Unity Movement another; some accepted race (as did the ANC in its four-spoked wheel), some rejected it, and some presented nationalist versions of race politics.[11]

The process of changing our belief system can be hard, painful, and protracted; and we often end up retaining invalid prior beliefs even while accepting new information. To do this, we build a mental firewall between the contradictory elements of the two sets of knowledge or belief, and only breach this barrier to reconcile opposing concepts when absolutely forced to do so. As Comins notes, writing about the retention of invalid scientific ideas:

> We humans are bundled contradictions. We are remarkably comfortable with conflicting beliefs. We draw conclusions using invalid reasoning and illogical, emotional gut feelings. We trust unreliable sources and act upon belief based on falsehoods that we once learned as gospel truth ... But is it enough? Is our acceptance of incorrect information, from which we build our views of the world, the best we can expect from life? I think we can do better.[12]

In this chapter I make a case for the necessity of thinking beyond the boundaries of common sense, of opening the issue of race to dialogue and debate, arguing that we have to and can do better. In Part One I drew attention to the difficulty we often experience in even imagining that there may be questions to be asked of the commonsense body of ideas within which we live. Here is an example of that discovery in a rather unexpected context, the journal *Astronomy*: "'Jimi Hendrix really opened up the heavens,' says [the ex-Queen guitarist and astronomer, Brian] May. "It's really hard to imagine the world without Jimi because he changed it so much. All of us thought we knew what guitar playing was. Jimi tore asunder all the limitations that none of us really knew were there."'[13] That is what common sense does: create the 'limitations that none of us ... [know are] there'.[14]

Intellectually, too, common sense as the basis of knowledge has implications. In response to critics of his denial of the existence of races, the philosopher Kwame Anthony Appiah argues that for some 'the erasure of the term "race"... simply threatens to leave too vast a discursive void'.[15] Race has become sense-making in many areas of life

– political, economic, social, even religious. What will we do when we find that the barbarians – a metaphor for that which seems to explain our predicaments – are not threatening at the gates, are not a reasonable source of our fears? Such fears do not provide the motivation and justification for our actions. Rather, their 'existence' has provided false answers to the serious issues we confront. Well, for a start we can kill the messengers that bring the supposedly good tidings of 'no threat'. But that is crude avoidance of having to confront the real challenges head-on.

Defamiliarising the familiar; disturbing the apparently fixed: that was what two intellectuals, each in his own way, did in response to the apparent solidity of the apartheid edifice. The one, Steve Biko, aimed his ideas of Black Consciousness at the population classified Native/ Bantu/Black, Indian and Coloured. The other, Rick Turner, directed an important part of his writing at apartheid's white Christians (as a group potentially open to reflecting on their personal moral dilemma – the injunctions of the Christian faith and their relationship to the dehumanising apartheid policy). In 1972 Turner wrote the book *The Eye of the Needle*, which was published in a series by the Study Project on Christianity in Apartheid Society. In it he argued:

> unless we can see our society in the light of other possible societies we cannot even understand why it works as it does, let alone judge it. Let us take the example of thinking about race. It is 'common sense' (to white South Africans) that black people are inferior to white people. And this common sense is not just some sort of delusion. It is based on white South Africans' experience of the objective 'inferiority' of most blacks in, for example, education, income, dress, and language proficiency (that is, proficiency in the only languages that whites recognise). And, moreover, nearly everyone they know treats blacks as inferior. They see black 'inferiority' as one of the imperatives of human nature. They 'explain' a social fact by direct reference to biology and thereby misunderstand it. If we assume the natural inferiority of a group we don't look for social causes of its actual 'inferiority'. If, on the other hand, we discover that there is no biological root for this 'inferiority', no imperative of human nature, then we begin to ask the illuminating question: What is the social structure that creates the various objective 'inferiorities' of certain groups? And only then do we understand how our society operates.[16]

There is much to be taken from this extract, asking for defamiliarising the familiar, and also from the very next sentence in the chapter: 'Common-sense thinking obscures reality.'

It is not only that utopian thinking offers a way out of the impasse of living in the world as it appears to have been intended. Utopian thinking, as a method, is also in itself a form of change in that it introduces the imperative for moral evaluation of actions and goals. Rick Turner's suggestion that we engage in the fascinating task of 'utopian thinking' is simple, but also challenging. Utopian thinking, in this case, is not a search for ways of escaping the present – it is a way of recognising and confronting the challenges that stand in the way of achieving goals on which we can agree. It is utopian in the sense of going beyond concessions and compromises, of rejecting the argument that 'there is no alternative' to what has thus far been chosen, and 'instead explor[ing] the absolute limits of possibility by sketching an ideally just society'.[17]

Turner confronted the reality of racist and sexist ideas. In response, he posited a utopian ideal of a world in which such ideas would not be held – would not make sense – and suggested how we could overcome the obstacles to thinking about the social world, in liberating ways. Utopian thinking outlines the features of the society we wish to create. Once we have these features in our sights we must work to understand the present society we live in, recognise the obstacles that must be overcome, and identify the practical tasks necessary to remove them:

> unless we think in Utopian terms about South African society we will not really come to understand how it works today. We will take for granted its inequalities, power relations and behaviour patterns which need to be explained. Nor will we be able to evaluate the society adequately. We will not understand on how many levels there are alternatives, and so the possibility of choice, and so the possibility of moral judgement.[18]

Implied in what Turner proposes is that such thinking is informed by certain values, a morality embedded in what we wish to achieve. It is a process imbued with ideas of the full realisation of what humans are capable of in our variety. Bauman too, referring to practices of categorisation, mentions the suspension of moral judgement as a consequence of the abstraction that underlies classification, the fixing of humans as specimens. He adds: 'Genocide differs from other murders in having a *category* for its object ... [It is] the kind of murder oblivious to differences of age, sex, personal quality or character.'[19] During the xenophobic murders in South Africa in 2008, the burning Mozambican man shown in televised images, Ernesto Alfabeto Nhamuavhe, was not an individual to those who set him alight, but a member of the category named *amakwerekwere*, the foreigners, those whose 'otherness' was betrayed by their accents (or their vaccination marks). When lesbian women are raped (for 'corrective' reasons) and murdered, or women accused of witchcraft are killed, their attackers do not care what the names of these victims are.[20]

The challenge lies in recovering an ethics that includes those made 'other', placed beyond the right to life, in our recognition of people who are 'like us'. Roberto Toscano, in his article addressing a 'philosophy of coexistence', says that 'violent conflicts are made possible only by the existence of partial ethics. The corollary is that only on the basis of nonpartial ethical approaches can differences and tensions be managed without recourse to group violence.' We have to define and embrace moral values that include all those around us, all of humanity. These moral values, once identified, can serve as that utopian goal towards which our existing thinking should be directed. As Toscano notes, the belief that 'we' are better than 'they' are makes 'us' deaf 'to the rights of others', a deafness 'that is sanctified, made mandatory'. Even those who are of us and wish to act in a different fashion will be compelled to act with the group. It explains how 'the individual's tendency to refrain from shedding the blood of others is overcome by group solidarity and its concomitant rationalizations'.[21]

We simplify everyday matters to the extent that they are meaningless in any quest for true understanding. Or else we elevate them to the unquestionable level of commonsense 'truths' which obscure more than they reveal. The world *is* complex. We may continue, at times cynically or, at best, uncritically, to use the terms denoting races and attribute essential behaviour to these categories. We probably claim attributes specific to our 'own race', either superior to or irreconcilably different from the characteristics we see in others. Thus the 'four spokes' of the South African population wheel form part of a 'whole', but each remains distinct, identifiable as 'other', marks of difference or diversity to be 'managed'. This, within the context of segregationist South Africa, is how most opposition movements, notably the ANC, understood the nation.

While an argument has been made here for doing away with race-based measures of redress, and the whole panoply of interventions that go along with it, the same involvement in race-based approaches to social problems is also the reason why sensitivity has to be shown to the role of race thinking in people's understanding of their humanity. Simplistic rejection of these ingrained ways of seeing the self will not help people to move beyond them. As Bauman reminds us, the 'meaning and significance' of race may extend beyond questions of dislike and hatred. While race thinking in itself is sufficient for racism to exist, the ways in which racist attitudes are confronted will vary. Issues of racism (and not only those that relate to criminal expressions of racial hatred) need to be addressed in an ongoing conversation and removed from the domain of crude claim and counter-claim, accusations and denials. This is not to argue that conversation has to accept all opinions, that all standpoints are valid.

Evidence of the urgent need to introduce disturbances of the everyday of categorical thinking is all around us, if we just care to notice it. In terms of scale and global spread, the most obvious instances are genocidal and other forms of ethnic and nation-based killings over the last century. The history of our subregion has not been exempt from extreme murderous actions directed against groups of people. Both race and ethnicity have been the basis for such killing in our political history, to suppress and to advance the struggle against racist apartheid. These actions should be enough to disturb our general complacency and fill us with horror at what we are capable of. We need not refer to social scientists!

NON-RACIALISM: EMPTY CLAIM IN THE PRESENT OR STEPS TOWARDS A FUTURE GOAL?

Non-racialism refers to the rejection of the use of race categories as apparently neutral, meaningful, 'natural' ways of distinguishing between humans according to perceived somatic similarities. It responds to the race thinking that informs social relations. It has the potential to serve as a challenge not only to the validity of the categories, but also to the inevitable attribution of certain essential characteristics to each 'race'. A non-racial society cannot simply be decreed into being or claimed to exist; it can only be progressively achieved through ongoing actions to challenge racial and racist practices. In a world exclusively founded on race thinking, the obstacles to non-racialism are everyday practices that must be overcome through a process of constant identification and struggle. Because of their everyday acceptance, they will have to be explored and identified deliberately in order to find other ways.

The notion of non-racialism is an example of utopian thinking: a moral goal that helps us explore the world in which we live, and search for practical ways of moving beyond it, towards a better world in which to be human. However, while the notion has the advantage of already being familiar in the minds of many South Africans, it also suffers from general misuse and abuse. It is already a commitment contained in something as real, effective and immediate as the 1996 Constitution,[22] even if it is at the same time as unreal as the contradictory and confusing claims of an 'unbroken thread' in the politics of the ANC. It is used as a political slogan, or a switch to be turned on by stating its existence; it is seen at times as a statement of fact used to hide continuing racism, to separate what 'we' stand for from what 'they' stand for. What I am suggesting is that the notion of non-racialism be rescued from these illusory or disingenuous uses, and restored to its function as an impossible goal. (In its very 'impossibility' lies its value. It is always a challenge.)[23]

Utopian thinking certainly needs to be extended, as Rick Turner proposed, to such core aspects of society as gender relations and the economic system, which we take for granted. But here I will keep to my primary focus on race and non-racialism, and set out what I see as four steps we need to take in moving towards this utopian ideal.

Step One is to disabuse ourselves of the idea that we have achieved a non-racial society, and even that we have a clear idea of what non-racialism is and that we know how to work actively towards such a state of being. Non-racialism should be presented as an ideal to which we can aspire, for reasons that are positive in themselves, as recognition of a shared humanity and commitment to social justice, and also as reaction to the negative, stultifying and hurtful effects of racialism and racism. It requires that we give theoretical and practical content to the concepts of racialism and racism, in order to arrive at a clear understanding of what non-racialism can mean. Step Two is to investigate the present, and recognise the status of race thinking and racism in practice, both at the level of common sense as well as in its institutionalised forms. Step Three demands the practical identification of present obstacles that stand in the way of progress towards the utopian ideal. This is a process that requires critical reflection on the world in which we find ourselves, and demands understanding and debating the past as well. Finally, Step Four involves proposing some practical measures, in order to create the atmosphere in which people can recognise the need for alternative ways of being and participating in social life. I will elaborate briefly what each of these steps entails.

Step One, then, is to explore and confirm that non-racialism does not exist, and never has in our country. In her book *Deconstructing Apartheid Discourse*, Aletta Norval discusses whether the notion of an Afrikaner *volkstaat* (people's state) would have a future hold in the post-1994 South Africa. She concludes that the viability of the idea of such an ethnically exclusive state will depend 'in the longer term ... on the degree to which non-racialism succeeds in providing a mechanism for drawing together the disparate elements of South African society'. She adds, optimistically, that 'it is only in the unlikely event of a total failure of that project that the gloomy scenario sketched by elements of the far right may become a reality'.[24] Her argument can be seen as an acceptance of the importance of non-racialism as a goal for the post-1994 government, one which could be sufficient to defeat demands for racial or ethnic separatism. However, such moves towards social solidarity have been sorely absent, not because of any white right-wing threat, but because of the deliberate maintenance of racialism within the political mainstream. We have to accept that non-racialism does not exist as an aim in any meaningful way, despite the multiple claims made for the term.

In brief, what is the history of the goal of non-racialism? Julie Frederikse makes a case for non-racialism as the driving force behind resistance to colonialism, segregation and apartheid.[25] I have previously argued that the 'unbroken' thread was, however, not non-racialism but in effect multiracialism, a vision of a shared polity and citizenship based on individuals as members of race groups.[26] As belief in the coming end of apartheid grew during the 1970s and 1980s, grounded on struggles that recognised other forms of identity (such as class), the term 'non-racialism' was brought to the fore with vigour, even if not always with clear content. Apparently, it seemed so obvious that there was no need to define it. Mostly it seemed to reflect a drawing of the 'races' together into the same organisations, which was already a step forward from the extreme separations manufactured by apartheid. In 1985, for example, a journalist asked Oliver Tambo, the exiled president of the still-banned

ANC, to distinguish the commitment to 'non-racialism' from the more familiar 'multiracialism'. His response appeared subsequently in the movement's journal *Mayibuye*. He said:

> There must be a difference. That is why we say non-racial. We could have said multi-racial if we had wanted to. There is a difference. We mean non-racial, rather than multi-racial. We mean non-racial – there is no racism. Multi-racial does not address the question of racism. Non-racial does. There will be no racism of any kind and therefore no discrimination that proceeds from the fact that people happen to be members of different races. That is what we understand by non-racial.[27]

From this early reflection, whose importance the organisation confirmed by publishing it in its own journal, the ANC left a legacy that equates non-racialism with either multiracialism (between people 'who happen to be members of different races') or non-racism ('non-racial – there is no racism'). Both of these interpretations are often stated directly or implied in the way the term is used, even today. In other words, the commitment to non-racialism has been present for many decades as a rallying cry or a description of organisations allowing multiracial membership.

This 'unbroken thread', now as a rejection of racialism as an organising principle of social life, was to be found not only in the ANC but also (and maybe even more strongly), as David Everatt argues, among white oppositional groups such as the Liberal Party.[28] However, where the commitment to non-racialism resided most deliberately and consistently was in the marginalised history of various smaller groups, of which the Unity Movement was the best known. We should heed the relevant call of Kelly Gillespie: 'I would like to read these less familiar trajectories of struggle as a rich archival seam that, despite going underground, so to speak, should be recovered for its potential to instruct our political present.'[29] The Unity Movement position was a radical approach, actively rejecting racism, and actively advancing ideas and practices that did not find a solution in multiracialism. Here, in the serious reflection and historical action based on such an understanding of non-racialism, lies a kernel of reawakening debate.[30]

Step Two is to investigate what forms of race-based practice and ideology exist, and what is promoted by government policies, if it is not non-racialism. I need not go into this at any length here, beyond referring the reader to my arguments in Part Two. We remain immersed in our racialised lives, and now not only because of the legacy of apartheid, but through the acceptance that this is the only way to continue, a 'necessary legacy' we must carry with us into the future, a legacy of the present. All of this brings us back to the need for a vision of a society that has moved truly beyond where we have been, beyond where we are now, and reaches constructively towards the utopian ideal of non-racialism.

Step Three in this process is to define the obstacles to the realisation of that utopian goal. The central obstacle is racialism and the race classification which it allows and even demands. Racialism, as we have seen, is the commonsense justification for race-based corrective action, for legislation and policy formulation, and consequently for the ether of race thinking within which we live. The challenge, then, is to investigate seriously how we can make non-racialism not just a largely meaningless commitment in the founding values in the Constitution, but something to strive for actively and in concrete ways.

Let me make a provocative claim: the constantly repeated phrase 'the legacies of apartheid' stands in the way of addressing imaginatively, innovatively, realistically, the enormous challenges of the present. This is not to make the absurd claim that there are no legacies. On the contrary, it is to say that those legacies are the problems of the now, and that blaming the past stands directly in the way of achieving resolution in the future. The dominant political mindset is allowed to find refuge in the past. And when the present is confronted – for example, through service delivery protest – it is not possible to see these confrontations as opportunities for constructive, imaginative exploration of solutions to problems that go far beyond the local, in a shared national and even global conversation.

In April 2013 Trevor Manuel, minister in the Presidency, made a claim similar to mine. Addressing a conference of senior civil servants, he certainly did not deny the effect of apartheid on the present (as he was immediately accused of doing); rather, he took issue with the government's failure adequately to confront immediate concerns about service delivery and take effective corrective action. Herein lay the problem: 'Nineteen years into democracy, our government has run out of excuses. We cannot continue to blame apartheid for our failings as a state … For almost two decades, the public has been patient in the face of mediocre services. The time for change, for ruthless focus on implementation has come.'

Interestingly, Manuel had introduced his talk by saying, 'Our challenge is to simultaneously build a non-racial society while taking steps to address the inequities of the past.'[31] The *Sunday Independent*, which reported his speech, ran a parallel comment from the general secretary of the National Education, Health and Allied Workers Union (NEHAWU), Fikile Majola, representing a large proportion of civil service workers. His and several other responses saw Manuel's appeal as denialism, and then attacked him as 'unaccountable to the ANC', wishing to 'operate as an independent maverick', 'as a super-minister' in a 'super-ministry', as presenting options no different from those of the opposition Democratic Alliance. Here was another example of the silencing of debate that characterises many interchanges in the post-1994 context.

Manuel was quite correct in linking non-racialism and equality – they should be inseparably part of that utopian goal. The former is not possible without the latter being effectively and visibly addressed, in a multitude of locations. However, as I have argued, it is not acceptable to define inequality in terms of incorrect racial demographics, and therefore to remedy inequality primarily through race-based policies. Success measured in these terms, for example in the extent to which a 'deracialised capitalism' has been achieved, is entirely fallacious, given that capitalism is the very system at the heart of inequality.

A second clear obstacle, related to the first, lies in the difficulty (even impossibility) of dislodging racialism, unless a remarkable number of coincidental factors occur. Appiah confronts this challenge when he writes, in an article whose focus is primarily on race thinking in the US, that 'the final repudiation of race as a term of difference' could be rejected by those who wish to hold on to racialism, on several grounds. First, on the ground that such rejection is incorrect, and that there are, in fact, biologically identifiable races, with specific attributes having meaningful social effect.

As a second ground, Appiah notes that it may be argued 'that a statement of this truth [that there are no races, other than what exist as social constructs] is politically inopportune'. However, he responds: 'I am enough of a scholar to think that the truth is worth telling and enough of a political animal to recognize that there are places where the truth does more harm than good. But, so far as the United States is concerned, I can see no reason to believe that racism is advanced by denying the existence of races.'[32]

This is an important point, that by denying the 'existence' of biological races (race as 'natural') one is denying the effects of the socially constructed existence of races, on which rest many arguments for the retention of race categories.[33] This is probably the most important argument that has to be confronted by any critic of race classification. However, I certainly agree with Appiah that those consequences are not all effectively the result of race discrimination, and that racialism is an inadequate base on which to construct redress; and that a race-based society carries the seeds of past and future conflict and ongoing humiliation and denigration. Such consideration must also take into account Appiah's example quoted above, which separates the struggle against racism from the retention of the notion of 'race'. Racialism is not *necessary* to combat racism but provides, rather, the very terms on which racism builds.

The third reason advanced for the retention of race thinking, not often expressed so clearly, is the perceptive one already referred to, that 'its absence simply threatens to leave too vast a discursive void'.[34] An everyday life without the simplifying (and comfortable) commonsense language of races, the prior vocabulary of groups into which we are born, is beyond easy grasp. How much will we have to shed, and explore and explain in alternative ways, if we reject the seeming obviousness of the existence of races; if we jettison the tremendous explanatory power that it offers in everyday life and in political and academic discourse? We are told that the barbarians threaten us, after all.

I invite the reader to try this experiment: deliberately avoid using any term that expresses or implies race for one day; avoid the use of the term 'they' to name others who have committed some misdemeanour – the 'they' usually implies members of some category (such as 'race'); note when you yourself turn to race thinking as the first port of call. Next, explore what was implied by your (near-) use of the race labels. Find another way of describing the 'they'; and see to what extent the attributes are not shared by all people, in both positive and negative implications. How much are we sacrificing by not taking the first small step in such a bold journey; a journey for which we need much more research and open debate to help us chart new paths?

The discourse of race carries massive weight, not only through overlapping with deep-rooted ideas and cultural practices, but also by seeming to answer fully the question of socio-economic inequality. But, as I have argued throughout this book, racism and inequality are not the same thing. Discrimination is not exploitation, even though discrimination may have material, and not just interpersonal, effects.

A further obstacle to initiating a journey towards the non-racial utopia (as a 'thought', an imagined, end-goal) lies in the public condemnation of behaviours that contradict notions of fixed categories, and even the sanctioning of violence against people identified as crossing such social boundaries as are believed to exist. These boundaries of fixed identity (whether sexual, gendered, racial, linguistic or any other) may be policed, for example, through notions of tradition, of religion, of social norms, through bureaucratic practices, or through cultural exclusion and mockery. Control of borders can happen in various ways, but the first step is to fix dominant forms of identity in language and thinking, to create very clear distinctions between 'us' and 'them' (no matter if this always presents an exaggerated or selective picture). In the process, not only are differences essentialised and presented as applying to all within the group, but this then allows for various forms of deviation to be identified as deliberate – and unacceptable – exceptions to the norm. Let me give an example: for Hendrik Verwoerd, minister of native affairs and later prime minister, there were deviants among white people, and deviants among black people. The former were easily identified in their calls for a franchise for all and the abolition of all separatist laws; the latter were 'detribalised natives'. Those who were urbanising and gaining western education, as distinguished from education appropriate to 'their own', were to be limited in number and returned to their tribal life. They were those 'who try to cross the border line of European life, to become traitors to their own people and to desert their own people'.[35]

In many cases those who break the rules of the category that define an 'us' are women, crossing the male-imposed boundaries of gendered behaviour, who are seen as traitors to their sex and sexuality and, hence, an affront to masculinity. Other familiar instances are those who by breaking the rules of belonging to 'the nation' call on themselves accusations of treason and lack of patriotism, even populist responses that can lead to violence, including rape and murder, as part of xenophobic cleansing. Just examine the various words employed for 'traitor' in the languages you speak, and then the number of situations in which they are used. Most of these will refer to a stereotyped group. In Afrikaans, for example, a traitor is a *verraaier*, and you could (during the apartheid years, and earlier) be a *lands-verraaier*, *volks-verraaier*, *taal-verraaier*, *ras-verraaier* (a traitor to country, nation, language, race) and so on; in each case, breaking the order of what is expected. Joha Louw-Potgieter, in her study of 'dissident Afrikaners', those crossing the boundaries of what is expected of members of that ethnic group, makes an important point: 'Those who have accepted uncritically the notion of the organic unity of "Afrikanerdom" inherent in the ideology of *volkseenheid* (an ideology of unity of the nation, propagated by Afrikaner nationalists since the 1940s in order to mobilize divergent Afrikaans speakers as "Afrikaners"), might have been blinded to the permeable boundaries and fragmented nature of this group.'[36]

We need reminders of these 'permeable boundaries' and the many crossings within, and from and into, any group. We need to recognise them when we see them, find them, acknowledge them, reward them when they exist, rather than enforce borders through word or deed. Njabulo Ndebele has wisely said:

> what we [as South Africans] do actually share is a sense of having in each one of us what the other is; it is the most common thing that all of us have across the country. But in a sense we have been rejecting the implications of this, because it seems that each of us, to various degrees, wants to hold onto some notion of purity that has not been tainted by the other. But in fact, it's not possible to find such purity.[37]

'Impure' is what we are and what we have always been, 'entangled' in a multiplicity of ways.

Similar boundary protection occurs in many other groupings in South Africa and in many other locations – for example, the 'group' that defines itself in terms of its heterosexuality and uses derogatory names and extreme violence to respond to the 'deviancy' of gays and lesbians. The 'coconut' label is applied to those, identified largely through their accent, who are seen to be black South Africans who have become 'white'; it is a label that rests on assumptions of purity and denies the admirable extent of cultural flexibility in South African society. And, of course, there are ethnic group boundaries, guarded by (male) 'traditional leaders', in large parts of South Africa, as there were under apartheid.

The belief in boundaries and the range of ways of protecting them – from brutal violence to name-calling and stereotyping – all serve to prevent open debate on non-racialism. Race, through its centrality, incorporates other distinct spheres of group identity: homosexuality is seen as unAfrican; culture is seen to be separated into African, Indian, Coloured and white cultures. And there is the deadly label of *amakwerekwere* applied to non-South Africans. In South Africa especially, race and culture are inextricably linked – culture has been essentialised through its link to racial distinctiveness.

I have noted that classification of fellow humans is hardly ever neutral. One of the characteristics of difference between races is that of cultural distinctions. The British political and gender theorist Anne Phillips has written a book provocatively called *Multiculturalism without Culture*, in which she argues that 'the failure to problematise culture has contributed to a radical otherness that represents people as profoundly different in their practices, values, and beliefs'.[38] And therein lies the concern to which I repeatedly return – the creation of perceptions that those not like us are 'profoundly different'. Phillips's approach to the task of 'problematising culture' is located within specific contexts – especially the UK and North America. However, she advances certain principles which speak generally to this concern.

In the first instance, she wishes to maintain 'the *relevance* of culture without making culture a *determinant* of action'.[39] Related to this are two further points: a stress on agency, and on recognising that individuals rather than groups are the bearers of culture. Individuals bear their uniqueness, as well as those characteristics they share with others with whom they voluntarily associate. Agency implies the right to choose which aspects of 'groupness' are valid to the individual. These individuals, located differently within culture, must claim the agency to define what is acceptable to them in terms of values and behaviour. Their decisions will relate to the degree to which they choose to exit from the prescriptions of the group that define what exists, what is desirable, and what is possible for all members of the group.

Phillips also stresses that there are commonalities, despite what appear to be extreme cultural differences between groups – Njabulo Ndebele's 'having in each one of us what the other is'. These commonalities have to be sought and acknowledged, as much as the differences are valued as (supposedly) uniquely defining of each group. Claims of essential differences between groups deliberately ignore what is shared among them: there are no pure, untainted, primordial essences that distinguish members of different groups from each other.[40]

But not all people are complicit, nor does all behaviour imply acceptance of racialism. Let me conclude this section by referring to countervailing tendencies, both formal and personal.

In its Preamble, the Constitution of South Africa states that the people of the country recognise the injustices of their past and 'believe that South Africa belongs to all who live in it, united in our diversity'. Further, the Preamble asserts that the Constitution has been adopted as the supreme law of the country so as to 'heal the divisions of the past and establish a society based on democratic values, social justice and fundamental human rights'. The Founding Provisions in the first chapter commit the nation to 'human dignity, the achievement of equality and the advancement of human rights and freedoms' and to 'non-racialism and non-sexism'. The Freedom Charter, too, made a statement, radical for the time, in words subsequently repeated in the Constitution, that 'South Africa belongs to all who live in it'. Yes, it did add the terms 'black and white', but this could be read as a statement that the shared 'belonging' was a rejection of what the apartheid ideologues had intended by those racial terms – as Black Consciousness proponents did two decades later.

To accept the utopia of a world beyond apartheid – a world which demands redefined terms of inclusion and dignity – imposes an enormous burden of reflection and action. Such an 'honour code', without race but with the retained goal of equality, with obligations to all, means accepting the dignity which is due to ourselves and others: 'it connects our lives together'.[41] The ideas of 'connecting', 'dignity', 'recognition', 'impurity' need desperately to be explored.

This is not an easy task. Ideas about another way of making sense of the social world of inequalities, life conditions and social power, of learning to live together not as 'races', are not just inserted into a void. These ideas have to compete, continuously, with the firmly embedded notions of the existence of 'barbarians', those raced others who seem to be essential for giving sense to our own existence, who provide the only mirror that confirms our own racialised identity. These ideas also have to compete with the race-populist mobilisation that is so enticingly available to politicians. And, finally, it has to compete with the state's template of race, a template that guides actions in a myriad of institutions and organisations and involves thousands and thousands in the bureaucracy of race classification.

It is not impossible. The utopian future of non-racialism has been formally stated (if we can recognise it as that, as a commitment in the

Constitution), has been claimed in small pockets and often silenced examples of shared relationships and spaces, in organisational commitments and practices, in exploration of other ways of tackling imperative social issues. This has been the case throughout the history of South Africa. Here, I am not referring to the crudities of 'rainbow-type' race relations advertising campaigns. I have in mind the ways in which people – especially young people – are exploring other ways of identifying themselves as social beings, despite the obvious obstacles they encounter. As Appiah writes, despite the difficulties, 'at the end of the moral revolution, as at the end of a scientific revolution, things look new. Looking back, even over a single generation, people ask, "What were we thinking? How did we do *that* for all those years?"'[42]

We make race, we make gender, we make fixed categories of culture, and because we make them we can unmake them, in our thinking and in our practices. It is not impossible.

There have always been other options for defining our individual and social identities as South Africans, despite the overarching historical narrative that has prioritised race. As Norman Etherington reminds us, there are 'histories which are less determined, more aware of multiple possibilities, histories which suggest life beyond the struggle against apartheid'.[43] They are there in the notion of shared class interests, in solidarity against gender oppression experienced by most women, and in movements and intellectual interventions that might have been shaped by already existing notions of race, but nevertheless had an origin in aspects of social life that lie outside race. These all have to be explored, understood, encouraged to expand their experiments in imagining and creating a non-racial reality.

Likewise, what might still be seen as 'alternative' ways of relating to others, forms of community, recognition of solidarities, experiences and goals that clearly transcend race, must be sought out, recognised, explored and supported. And here, the promise of a different kind of socialisation through education, and the opportunity offered to children of a different way of being once grown up in a new South Africa, need urgently to be introduced, cherished and attended to. This is how Njabulo Ndebele recently put it:

> Hamlet's question, 'to be or not to be?' comes back to us in at least two
> ways: in the first, 'to be' is to exist; in the second, it is 'to become'. Right

now, 'to be' in South Africa is to take up the historical imperative 'to become'. It is to enter other identities without necessarily abandoning the grounded-ness of one's received identity. But that identity could have many layers: family, community, church, school, peers, soccer club, in various strengths of influence and impact.

For many in South Africa the political identity has over-determined the potential of their multiple grounded-ness. It has tended to lead them to the choice not to connect with others who have no familiarity from past associations. In hindering the expansion of awareness and the opportunities for co-created identities it has nurtured the politics of the blunt instrument.[44]

Of course, such alternatives, such 'becomings', are threatening to the existential security of many. But, to borrow a challenge expressed by Edwin Cameron, a Constitutional Court judge and gay rights activist, we cannot allow external and internal stigmatisation to silence us. The issue of racialism carries within it the danger of narrowing our life chances, of shaping society for the worse, of creating and maintaining divisions, the implications of which are too horribly clear to ignore.

Utopian thoughts and voices, ways of thinking that can take us out of the dangerous dead end of race thinking, also underlie Paul Gilroy's call for a 'planetary humanism' and Kwame Appiah's 'cosmopolitanism' – both writers to whom my argument for a utopian vision owes much.[45] Appiah opened up another way of reflecting on the everyday, and on the variety that is Africa, in his book *In My Father's House*, a work which shows how it is possible to think against the grain of much commonsense race thinking in present-day South African political discourse.[46] Gilroy, more recently, has asked the same questions about race and racialism in *Against Race*.

What is interesting in both these cases is that the authors clearly distinguish between race thinking (or racialism, as Appiah calls it) and racism, and have had to defend their rejection of race-based politics against those who say that their arguments do an injustice to the fight against racism, harming that noble struggle. Paul Gilroy has said: 'The political will to liberate humankind from race-thinking must be complemented by precise historical reasons why these attempts are worth making.' He continued:

The first task is to suggest that the demise of 'race' is not something to be feared. Even this may be a hard argument to win. On the one hand, the beneficiaries of racial hierarchy do not want to give up their privileges. On the other hand, people who have been subordinated by race-thinking and its distinctive social structures (not all of which come handily color-coded) have for centuries employed the concepts and categories of their rulers, owners, and persecutors to resist the destiny that 'race' has allocated to them and to dissent from the lowly value it placed upon their lives.[47]

Paul Gilroy returned to the notion of 'racial hierarchy', but now linked to 'human rights', in his book *Darker than Blue*. Here, he takes issue with the manner in which 'the political idea of human rights acquired a particular historical trajectory ... [in which] its progressive development is often told ritualistically as a kind of ethno-history', a history in which the 'blood-saturated histories of colonisation and conquest are rarely allowed to disrupt that triumphalist tale'.[48] Instead, Gilroy argues for an 'alternative, critical approach requir[ing] seeing not just how all-conquering liberal sensibilities evolved unevenly into considerations of human rights, but how a range of disputes over and around the idea of universal humanity – its origins, its hierarchies, and varying moral and juridical dispositions – were connected to struggles over race, slavery and imperial rule'.[49] He continues later:

It turns out that struggles against racial hierarchy have contributed directly and consistently to challenging conceptions of the human. They have valorised forms of humanity that are not amenable to colour coding, and in complicating our approach to human sameness they may even have refused the full, obvious force of natural difference articulated as both sex and gender. These struggles have not only been utopian in character.[50]

Utopias, as social systems, are not easily achieved – in fact, let us be honest, they are not achievable. However, utopian thinking does place an alternative vision on the agenda for debate. But it goes beyond that. Such thinking exercises the mind, that much neglected organ within rigid and essentialist thinking, and also presents us with the challenge of searching for ways to go beyond the race thinking and race-based societies within which we live. I have referred to the banal practice of form-filling, as confirmation of the existence of races. Here is how Appiah formulates a challenge to that one pervasive method of reinforcing race thinking:

> Were the government to modify these practices, it would remove at least one tiny strut that gives support to the idea that social conceptions of race are consistent with reality: the fact that the state appears to be able to construct successful practices that assume that social conception. Such a modification could be motivated in many ways (not least by the recognition that the relevant social conceptions *are* rationally defective). But it might, surely, also be motivated by the thought that government action here could help to reshape – or, anyway, diminish the salience of – racial identities in ways that would lessen their self-conflicting character.[51]

Small steps, perhaps. But how much influence they would have on the everyday practices of millions of people.

In the next chapter I turn to Step Four in the process of journeying towards the ideal of a non-racial future – the practical measures we need to take to bring this future closer.

6

Now that there are no barbarians?

Cavafy's poem speaks to all of us:

> And now what will become of us without Barbarians? –
> Those people were some sort of solution.

What happens, then, if I have managed to convince the readers of this book that 'there is no need for employing race'? What if, therefore, the need for resistance to racialism is accepted, as much as it is to racism; if the questions I and many others before me have raised about the disturbing direction taken in post-1994 South Africa, based on the embrace of race thinking, are appropriate? What if we recognise that we have allowed racialism, as well as similar forms of othering, to continue to such an extent that it can override the demeaning experiences and memories of apartheid, and deny the real consequences of race thinking, the dehumanisation and mass extermination of fellow human beings? What if we acknowledge that the apparent answer that race thinking has provided in so many circumstances is not a source of answers, but the very problem?

It is time to imagine the measures we can take to come closer to the utopian ideal of a non-racial society. Achievement is only in the imagining. My argument has been that to address racism – largely the actions of identifiable individuals or of an indefinable 'institutional' presence – leaves racialism unexamined and always present as the bedrock on which racism is built.

Non-racialism is the active undermining of the notions that natural groups, races, are the obvious building blocks of social order, and the basis of what constitutes difference (what we euphemistically call 'diversity' or 'multiculturalism') among human beings. This means, in the most basic terms, that non-racialism denies the existence of races, other than in the many forms in which we have created them, and works towards a social world in which a shared humanity, rather than difference, is the basis, the starting point, for interaction and action.

As personal experience has taught us, belief in the existence of races is in large part maintained through our shared collusion in perpetuating this belief, our own race thinking. We are complicit, and without our complicity the hold it has over us would weaken and, ultimately, fail. We are not confronting metal bars, unbreachable borders here. Raising questions about or even rejecting the obvious framework of ideas within which we live can be unsettling and even terrifying, but it does not kill or maim.

What I offer below are some reflections on where and how the process of working towards an equitable and non-racial society may be explored in thinking and in doing. I do not say 'may be achieved' – that would be a presumption of which I am not capable. This cannot ever but be the task of all South Africans, as citizens and human beings, and centrally also the task of a government in power.

REFLECTION: A MORAL REVOLUTION

It may well be that the commitment to non-racialism opens the door to social activism informed by Appiah's argument for an 'honour code' to achieve 'moral revolutions'. What does Appiah mean by this? He explains his approach to morality as 'ultimately practical ... about what we do'; hence, 'a moral revolution has to involve a rapid transformation in moral *behavior*, not just in moral sentiments'.[1] But why should the cases he draws on – duelling in Britain, foot binding in China, slavery in the US south – be 'moral revolutions'? Appiah says that he was surprised to find that 'honour' played a role in each one of these extensive social changes, which he then links to the role of social identities and the need for recognition, for status and respect ('We human beings *need others* to respond appropriately to who we are and to what we do').[2] Race classification seems to have blinded those in power to a point as obvious as this – the 'need' and the 'appropriate' response.

In all the varied cases Appiah examines, 'arguments against each of these practices were well known', but the practices continued and were deemed to be obvious and honourable, at least by those practising them, until they were done away with, because the 'respect' that had once been attached to them was removed in favour of another 'honour code'. Another order had superseded the one in existence, and there was no longer respect for those engaged in what had been accepted. For Appiah, having honour 'means being entitled to respect', an 'entitlement' that resides in honour codes. 'Dignity is a form of honor, too, and *its* code is part of morality.'[3] Respect is what you grant those who meet the standards of the code; contempt is what you show them if they do not. Those who fail to live up to the requirements of the 'honour code' of racialism have borne labels such as *verraaier* (under apartheid) and 'coconut' (post-1994). They may even no longer deserve to live, or live with 'us', whose code of group belonging has been broken.

Is the idea of societal change that comes through considering honour codes, ones relevant to abandoning race classification in South Africa, worth exploring? It would seem to me to be so. We will, in the first instance, have to remind ourselves of the defence offered for continuing with race classification in South Africa – the unexpected post-apartheid honour code of racialism. These arguments call on moral values and goals – of equality and redress, for defeating the legacies of apartheid – as motivation and justification. Race classification, by implication (because it is not called that), has been made honourable. But that does not make it moral. We will, then, have to recognise ourselves as moral beings with moral obligations, and racial classification as immoral, for the reasons I have advanced or for others: political, economic, religious, human. That leaves the issue of an alternative, less sectional moral honour code to be sought after.

There is a potentially home-grown morality that can form the core of an inner honour code based on human dignity rather than racial justification. It is to be found in the traditions of 'the struggle' in its many forms, of commitment to 'revolution', in the Freedom Charter and other similar documents, in religious principles, in the Constitution, in what 'post-apartheid' should mean. But then there has to be the courage to recover these terms from the definitions given to them by a single party, the ANC, on the basis that this party represents all, or at least all who are 'us'. The definitions that are at present applied, and the practices that flow from them, are exclusive of anything that is not linked to the dominant movement. The term 'democracy', if extended to include the goals of social justice too, offers such an honour code. The 'others' who could give recognition to such a code are, in this case, us – all of us, and not just the accepted spokespeople for the ideas necessary to shape an honour code directed against race classification. If we are all complicit in maintaining racialism, then non-racialism as a code cannot come into being without all of our efforts and commitments and demands.

REFLECTION: BORN AFTER RACE

Another meaningful possibility, if it is allowed to flourish, lies in the ways of life being created by the generation that has not experienced apartheid directly, those who were born after 1990. They are the ones who will draw their socialisation from what exists around them in a post-1994 country and from the way in which the past is presented. They are the first generation which does not necessarily seek recognition in a specific notion of 'the struggle', but in the wider challenges of creating a truly post-apartheid society. They also have to confront problems that are immediate – unemployment, poverty and inequality, poor education, HIV and other diseases – and not lived as the legacy of apartheid. They need not find refuge in the past, but can nonetheless accept challenges in the present. They could be enabled to engage in such exploration and participation, and in many cases they are. Or they could have the burden of the past, along with its responsibilities – but now expressed as guilt (of not having been part of it as their parents were, of not having 'struggle credentials') – placed on them. And there is a burden, of not having actually been there, and hence of memories that should be respected without question.

Eva Hoffman captures that complex of possibilities and burdens borne by 'the next generation' very well in calling it the lives lived 'after such knowledge'. In her case, that knowledge was of the Holocaust – she was born immediately after World War II. This is how she concludes her reflections:

> And indeed, the Holocaust continues to stand as a kind of limiting condition of experience, and therefore, a necessary part of our knowledge about human nature ...
>
> And yet, unless we want to fall into permanent melancholia or nihilistic

despair, we cannot take the Holocaust as the norm that governs human life. We cannot start from it as a basis … That is why it is necessary to separate the past from the present and to judge the present in its own light … For the inheritors of traumatic historical experience, the ability to separate the past from the present – to see the past *as* the past – is a difficult but necessary achievement.[4]

Of course, we live in a racialised country, with legacies and memories of the past. But already we do so in ways far removed from apartheid, with far greater complexity and variety of experiences and challenges that shape those memories – as lived and as represented. On the other hand, social conditions allow race thinking most of the time to inform and continue to 'make sense' of present experience. If the present fails to provide a dignified life, in its basic forms, or one shaped by the promises of a consumer society, then race is there, given credibility all the time by the state, available to justify 'failure' and to motivate for claims. Granting the new generation 'permission' to be something that the previous generation were not gains importance, because it will at the very least introduce flexibility in identity formation. Establishing and debating a moral honour code with a vision beyond racialism will grant them that permission to accept the challenge of moving past race in finding solutions appropriate to their causes. The space presented through utopian thinking is what should be the goal, not the simplicity of the obvious. Eva Hoffman's challenge, 'to see the past *as* the past … a difficult but necessary achievement', is our challenge too.

REFLECTION: EVER-CHANGING COLOUR

In Chapter 1, mention was made of the somatic base that skin colour provides as the main, though certainly not the only, indicator of racial distinction. The cases discussed earlier, such as the teachers confused about how to allocate pupils to racial categories, the classifiers at the university, the census agent who looked at me and 'self-classified' for me, relied in the first instance on appearance. If this did not work because appearances confused the apparent simplicity of the task, or because the classified subject refused to accept the category, then other indicators were used to prove what was suspected or to swing the decision one way or the other: surname, place of residence or school, accent, hair, language and so on.

But in general, the subtleties of four (or more) different race categories can be resolved into the simplistic binary of 'black' and 'white' races. On the other hand, one can follow Nina Jablonski, who challenges popular notions of colour and race in her book *Living Color*, and deny the apparent fixedness of skin colour, once the evolutionary clock is put in motion, or human sexual activity alters shades from generation to generation, or chemical means are employed, or tanning does the job – or if our own constructions of meaning change.[5] To give meaning to colour in the present, as a marker of race, is to remove the term from its history and from its place. The confusions created by using such an indicator should alert us to the general confusion that accompanies race classification, but the 'black and white' approach is too firmly part of our confident simplifications to cause real puzzlement. Roxanne Wheeler's fascinating exploration of 'categories of difference' in eighteenth-century Britain shows clearly how notions of 'socially relevant' indicators change over time. She notes, for example, that 'skin color and race as we know them today have not always been powerful tools to convey difference. At various times in European history, they have fostered meanings incongruent with the current ubiquitous conviction of their significance to identity.'[6]

Undermining the perception that colour equals race, disseminating the accurate story of skin colour differences, of evolution, of the varieties of difference globally, has to be a first step in the struggle against racialism. This needs to happen even if just to address race thinking in its simplistic form, and to stimulate the first moments of doubt and questioning in people's minds.[7]

REFLECTION: THE EVOLVING SCIENCE OF RACE

Mention was made earlier of the tremendous influence that science (and social science) had on the consolidation of race thinking and race practice. It was so powerful that the term 'scientific racism' has been attached to the fascination with finding proof on and in the body for the existence of distinctive races, through description, ascription, measurement, genealogies, and social scientific data-gathering. While these practices can best be illustrated with reference to the nineteenth century, they certainly did not end there.[8] The linkage between health and the racialised body, for instance, continues to this day. In 2013 the South African statistician-general, Pali Lehohla, released health figures from the General Household Survey and linked these, and even 'happiness' as a description of good health, to race categories.[9]

Even the field of genetics, where scientific breakthroughs have frequently been cited to dispel any confidence in notions of biological races, is still used to make racial claims. Zimitri Erasmus comments: 'These articulations of "Khoi-San-ness" and "Jewish-ness" as primarily biological, are key examples of what I call "throwing the genes". They indicate it is not sufficient simply to remind humans that there is no such thing as a Jewish gene, a KhoiSan gene, or an African gene. Instead it is important to ask: Why are biocentric meanings of "race", social identification and belonging so resilient?'[10]

Paul Gilroy makes claims for the effectiveness of genetic science in undermining notions of race, but expresses caution in his call for action. He starts the first chapter of his book *Against Race* with a quotation from Richard Lewontin: 'It is certainly not the case that our biology is irrelevant to social organization. The question is, what part of biology is relevant?' Gilroy's argument is against 'raciology' – 'the lore that brings the virtual realities of "race" to dismal and destructive life'.[11] Gilroy notes that race thinking has changed since the eighteenth and nineteenth centuries, under the influence of the reconstruction of the 'relationship between human beings and nature ... [under] the impact of the DNA revolution and of the technological developments that have energized it'. His book is 'premised upon the idea that we must try to take possession of that profound transformation and somehow set it to work against the tainted logic that produced it'. The 'crisis of "race" and representation, of politics and ethics, offers a welcome cue to free ourselves from the bonds of all raciology in a novel and ambitious abolitionist project'.[12] He had earlier warned his readers that this part of his book 'has a tone, but that should not disguise its practical purpose'.[13] Indeed, scientific racism was (and remains in some instances) a project. The authors I mention here all draw attention to the practical side, the process of combating race thinking and racism. Even utopian thinking, as Eddie Webster remarks, quoting a poem by Cavafy, is a practical process.[14] I could not agree more.

The process requires exploring and identifying the complex relationship between scientific knowledge and its effect and use in everyday life, specifically in relation to the role that such 'facts' play in informing, confirming and changing minds. Here are some further examples of what is called for.

Wilmot James, in *Nature's Gifts*, discusses the genetic language of life and devotes a chapter to skin colour;[15] a matter of central concern to Nina Jablonski as well.[16] James refers to the tragic case of Sandra Laing to illustrate the many 'lives that were wrecked' through that policy. Rasmus Winther and Jonathan Kaplan note that genomic data have had an effect on how people try to construct and reconstruct race.[17] They conclude that 'political agendas, social programmes, and moral questions premised on the existence of naturalistic race should accept that no scientifically grounded racial ontology is forthcoming, and adjust presumptions, practices and projects accordingly'.[18] Karen Fields and Barbara Fields discuss the manner in which genetics has come to play a role in the new racial order – despite evidence to the contrary.[19] What they wish to take from the book by J Craig Venter, the mapper of the genome, is that 'race' does not appear in the index, because he rejects the 'anti-individualism' that some commentators make of genetic results: 'When questions arose about his [Venter's] decision to take ... Human Genome Project's five samples from individuals who differed by what Americans call race, he replied that the point was to "help illustrate that the concept of race has no genetic or scientific basis".'[20]

REFLECTION: NO SOLUTION BUT US

Maybe what I am asking for here is close to the 'conversation' referred to by Michael Chapman in his book *Art Talk, Politics Talk* and by Kwame Appiah in *Cosmopolitanism*. My argument, after all, is that there is no solution but us. As Appiah puts it, in discussing the 'human in humanity': 'One connection – the one neglected in talk of cultural patrimony – is the connection not *through* identity but *despite* difference'.[21] What is required here is conversation, '[used] not only for literal talk but also as metaphor for engagement with the experiences and the ideas of others ... Conversation doesn't have to lead to consensus about anything, especially not values; it's enough that it helps people get used to one another.'[22]

Chapman, in a chapter titled 'South/North conversation', writes: 'We are reminded of comparison continuing to produce anxiety. Instead of transcending the divide of the colonial, or colonised, experience, argument continually re-inscribes the dichotomy. Instead of centres and edges finding open conversation between different understandings, different vocabularies, and different cultural paradigms, antagonists remain locked in reactive responses.'[23]

I am trying to engage in that debate, open the conversation, firstly with my own thoughts, but also with the society I live in, with the students I have taught, with related ideas in other places and other disciplines, and with alternative visions of future societies. Several South African commentators have called for a 'thinking' citizenry – we desperately need that in this field. The related challenge is to find ways of bringing people into conversation and not just into proximity. We need to create situations that demand engagement with each other. Those engagements certainly need not (should not?) be based on predefined difference and conflict, but may more constructively be entered into on the basis of shared problems (of which racism will be one, as will corruption, poverty, inequality, patriarchy, the environment and food production, deaths on the roads, HIV/AIDS, abuse and murder of children, illiteracy, etc.).

REFLECTION: WALKING AGAINST MARCHING

The struggle against apartheid was expressed so often in the form of walking, processions, wakes, protests. The gathering by women at the Union Buildings in Pretoria, the symbolic seat of Afrikaner power, in 1956 illustrates this point. They were there to protest against the extension of the pass laws to women as well as men. This was one of the high points in early protest action and is often referred to as a stirring example of 'walking in protest'.[24]

During my active lifetime I have participated in or closely observed many such walks: protests at the University of Natal against the banning of student leaders and educational segregation in the 1960s and 1970s; marches by thousands of workers during the 1973 strikes. Later, in 1976, at the University of the Witwatersrand we publicised the June 16 marches by pupils in Soweto; and joined the procession at the funeral of Neil Aggett, a trade unionist who died while in police detention in

1982. And then there was the gathering of probably more than 200,000 people when Nelson Mandela spoke in Durban in February 1990 after his release from prison, and called for weapons to be thrown into the sea to end the violence between Inkatha and ANC supporters. No public transport could cater for so many, so tens of thousands people walked to the venue.[25]

All of these marches and walks knew no race as a formative aspect. They were driven by a sense of solidarity with those protesting against their own oppression and the system at the heart of it, rather than by a desire to express race affiliation. All, therefore, went against the practices of separation, especially of race and space, that formed the basis of apartheid. Those who welcomed Mandela did so in the spirit of belief in a post-apartheid social and political world. It confirmed the inevitability of the end of apartheid and of the power of those present of all colours. In a way, a 'utopia' was closer at that moment.

There is a distinction between walking and marching that also applies to the deliberate effects of classification. This is how Rebecca Solnit describes walking, whether in protest or to commemorate solemn events: 'Such walking is a bodily demonstration of political or cultural conviction and one of the most universally available forms of public expression. It could be called marching, in that it is common movement toward a common goal, but the participants have not surrendered their individuality as have those soldiers whose lockstep signifies that they have become interchangeable units under an absolute authority.' She adds: 'Instead [walking protests] signify the possibility of common ground between people who have not ceased to be different from each other, people who have at last become the public.'[26]

Solnit is writing here about the US, but her general point invites reflection about the South African experience. She remarks: 'Citizenship is predicated on the sense of having something in common with strangers, just as democracy is built upon trust in strangers. And public space is the space we share with strangers, the unsegregated zone.'[27] With our race obsession in South Africa we need to think of shared space much more widely. If nearly 80 per cent of the population have to answer to being 'black African', what would the 'correct demographics' be in social space? In 2012 the newspaper *Die Burger* printed a graphic representation of South Africa's 'averageville', with its 100 inhabitants: 76 black, 12 white, 10 brown and 2 Indian.[28] Here is a clear 'legacy of apartheid', and the class structure that accompanied the racialised allocation of space. Why are so many public spaces zones to be feared or avoided because they have become places of discomfort or threat, rather than sources of potential pleasure? The answer lies in formal and informal practices of dividing, of stereotyping, of classification – public spaces take on a racialised character, or a masculinist atmosphere, just as people do, in a society subject to these practices. Sharing space, in the way described by Solnit, overcomes those divisions, even if just for the moment of protest action or during recreation – and in so doing gives people a sense of a different normality. Sharing space is, in the first instance, using space without fear – whether you are black, white, a woman, a child, disabled. Then people can interact, freely and with recognition rather than fear of other humans.

Inequality and poverty, the real curses in South Africa, have controlled the shaping of space for purposes of segregated housing – whether on class or racial grounds – rather than for any wider social goal.[29] Space used to further the goal of dignity for all – through provision of housing and services – is inextricably linked to visions of the path towards non-racialism. This, therefore, is another obstacle, a real apartheid legacy written on the ground, that needs to be tackled if we are to move towards that utopian vision. Apartheid physically separated people on the basis of race and ethnicity, and filled those spaces with cultural identities, with specific types of houses, signs and statues, and names, and with practices, structures and agents of social control. We live in the aftermath of that separation. Millions of people remain contained within those spaces under cultural management and differentiation ('traditional authorities') or subject to class-enforced divisions.

In the city where I live, Durban, deliberate attempts are being made in certain city suburbs to recover safe public space in parks. While their use still reflects the dominant space allocation through apartheid's Group Areas Act, and the manner in which class now throws its shadow over that, it is also increasingly shaped by the recreational opportunities these parks offer to all.

Many South Africans still patrol public space against identifiable groups who break the rules of what is expected of them as specimens of categories or prey on those specimens – non-South Africans, gays, women in pants and women generally, ethnic or racial others, to name just a few. Of course, there are still examples where people become 'the public', united in their moral outrage, but not in an enduring way. Sport, much acclaimed as a social unifier, does bring people together, but only to separate them again afterwards. Class has become the new divider of note: houses for the poor are still built in separate areas, and those who live in areas previously set aside for black people can only with great difficulty leave them to enter the more cosmopolitan spaces of the inner city, the leisure facilities, the middle-class consumer centres, because of the prohibitive costs of travelling.

This makes shared spaces, whether these are residential neighbourhoods, schools, sports facilities, parks, workspaces – all spaces where people can walk together, whatever the purpose may be – of such immense importance, visually and socially, in creating a truly post-apartheid South Africa.

REFLECTION: FOCUS ON CORE PROBLEMS, WITHOUT OLD ANSWERS

Denying a biological and fixed notion of race is not denying the problems that the use of race thinking is meant to address. In fact, this notion is one of the problems, one of the dangerous overlays that give existing social and economic problems a vicious twist. Race hides the true nature of most of the problems with its seeming simplicity and obviousness as simultaneously problem (legacy) and answer (race-based redress and divisive political mobilisation). The real concerns facing South Africa need to be dealt with not by maintaining divisions, certainly not of race. These are concerns affecting all of us, not just the poor or the discriminated against or, most fundamentally, the exploited. Making it the problem of race makes it the problem of the other and denies our involvement. Poverty and inequality are present, because there are the privileged, the rich. Inequality is the articulation of the 'causes' of wealth and of poverty. Women and children are raped, because there are men who do it. Foreigners are available as scapegoats, because of the nation-state. The environment is ruined, because we all, in our different ways, contribute to it or do not notice what others are doing – and the state, reflecting dominant interests, is lax in its protection on behalf of us, and mostly supports private exploitation of natural resources.

What is striking is how 'poverty' and 'the poor' are presented as discrete items, removed from the relational term 'inequality'; and then how 'inequality' is removed from a causal or even weakly linked relationship to wealth, to processes, to choices. Instead it is used as a technical measuring instrument, serving to disconnect the structural accumulation of wealth from the process of creating it. A good example comes from Statistics South Africa's latest General Household Survey, which blandly reports that in South Africa today 'four out of ten ... households rely on social grants as their only source of income ... The percentage of South Africans dependent on grants more than doubled in 10 years, from 12.7% in 2002 to 29.6% last year.'[30] We read this information together with media reports of the many examples, presented without comment, of gross conspicuous consumption and rewards handed out to those at the top. We should not read these items as disconnected; and we should not stop thinking about the ANC government's commitment to a 'deracialised' capitalism as the basis of South Africa's future.

We also need to question the use of race-based policies to redress inequality. A useful guide in this respect is Kanya Adam's book *Colour of Business*, which provides a good overview of affirmative action in such countries as the US and Malaysia. While acknowledging the argument made by proponents of affirmative action that such policies are a 'means to attack inequalities generated within an exclusivist society', she concludes that 'the race-based group rationale that since all blacks suffered discrimination, all require redress, obscures the fundamental question of which individuals within the group really benefit'.[31] 'Race-based affirmative action does not seek to eliminate class distinctions, but facilitates the acquisition of wealth by an already privileged enclave.'[32] She adds that 'one of the greatest inherent risks of affirmative action lies in nurturing the same racial divide which underpinned apartheid'.[33]

What is needed by way of 'racial redress' is something quite different, as Adam Habib and Kristina Bentley argue:

> Applying a contextual rational lens to an alternative [to race-based] redress programme in South Africa would lead to the conclusion that not only would black citizens be privileged, but also its poor and disadvantaged sections would be prioritised ...
>
> Such a redress programme would have to be constructed on alternative

'objective' criteria, ones that do not reinforce the historical divides within the society, and are compatible with a cross-section of citizens' views on what constitutes 'fair' and 'just'.[34]

Habib and Bentley provide examples of deliberate attempts to explore current policies and practices and, importantly, to suggest alternative forms of tackling poverty, inequality and some sense of a moral and inclusive social world.[35]

A last example can be found in the field of sport, where the causes of the repeated failure of affirmative action to make substantive changes to the composition of national and regional teams are easily identifiable. I must add, however, that the desire to participate in any one sport is certainly not evenly spread across such groupings as races – far too many variables enter to expect that – and needs to be acknowledged. The ex-international rugby player, radio presenter and columnist, John Robbie, succinctly makes the point of starting early in attempts to ensure potential sporting success for all:

> Comrade Gwede Mantashe [secretary-general of the ANC] was not just content to be a fan when talking the other day about rugby and the Springboks. He fancies Elton Jantjies [a top rugby player, categorised as Coloured] and loaded his comments with the race card.
>
> Get your government to kick-start real development and the top will look after itself, Gwede.[36]

By having contact with what happens on the ground, and travelling the byways of South Africa, the truly interested sports official will see how the overwhelming majority of South African children are deprived of even the minimum of sports facilities. That overwhelming majority includes also black children from rural and poor areas. As Liz McGregor has shown, the narrow range of factors that help ensure success are simply not available to most South Africans.[37] The same applies to all sporting codes, especially those that need playing fields and expensive equipment. Without wishing to diminish the magnitude of the task, the solutions are fairly obvious to identify and implement in such a way that all citizens of good will can see the sense and wish to participate.

REFLECTION: CLASS, CAPITALISM AND NON-RACIALISM

Here lies the essence of the issue – discrimination versus exploitation; race versus class. It is not possible to identify obstacles in the way of progress towards the utopian vision of non-racialism, and of the equally utopian vision of equality and dignity, without confronting capitalism – its effects in the past and its effects now. I have referred to this issue, of race and class, at several points in the book already. What global capitalism, in its local variant, has brought us since 1990 is an abstract non-racialism of consumerism. Move into the income brackets where at least some of the goals of consumerism and display of wealth can be met, and there you will find something that trumps race or is interwoven with race.[38] Look at the bizarre world created by global capitalism, where desired and envied products cannot ever be consumed by the vast majority, while being presented through the mass media as within everyone's reach, and you see frustration and warped aspirations. That version of a shared world does nothing to reduce inequality. Instead, it rests on it, structurally maintains and aggravates it, and can manifest itself in the most bizarre ways at the extremes of South African poverty. At the one end, there is the deliberate destruction, by youngsters who certainly cannot afford it, of the most expensive clothing to indicate an ability to consume when it clearly is not there;[39] and, at the other end, the most disgusting displays of wealth by those who have made it, and who also flaunt their political connections as if these are just so many more demonstrations of their material success. The link between the politics of entitlement and wealth is firmly established. The role model is hardly ever the committed civil servant, the dedicated teacher, the selfless nurse, the rural doctor.

In 2004, Ferial Haffajee, then editor of the *Mail & Guardian*, discussed the necessity for corrective action and the challenge to find alternative approaches. In response to what she referred to as an 'entire recruitment industry [which] has been born to poach "affirmative action" (AA) appointments from one company to another', she innovatively proposed that 'after one equity appointment, young black men and women should then refuse other equity-based appointments and even promotions. This will show that one leg up is all we need – thereafter we compete equally because we are as good. A meritocracy, a non-racial society is after all the desirable outcome of policies chosen and it should come sooner rather than later.' She ended her discussion with the following call: 'It's time to move beyond the sterile debate and name-calling that employment equity has become. It is time to move beyond easy celebrations and quick-fix appointments. The transfer of wealth is essential and imperative – the debate now is to determine how it will be exercised en masse and in substantial ways; not about whether we should do it or not.'[40]

Haffajee's 'substantial ways' do not include dispersing the right to exploit people's labour power through 'deracialising the economy'. A 'decent life' should not come to some individuals at the expense of other lives – that is, it should not be sustained by practices of exploitation and the benefits that flow from that, nor by seeing fellow humans as 'foreigners' who stand in the way of one's prosperity.

As Friedman and Erasmus note, there has been a changing relationship between class and race, in part due to state policy but probably mostly as a result of the transition to a democratic society, 'one in which a simple correlation between "race" and equity is not tenable, as it might have been in the heyday of apartheid'. 'One obvious implication is that demands for racial redress do not automatically challenge poverty.'[41]

> Indeed ... these forms of [race-based] redress ... will enhance the assets of higher income groups within racial categories while leaving those at the bottom untouched ... Another [implication] is that generalised measures to tackle poverty will not benefit all members of any racial group and will, in principle, be available across 'race'. Social reality and conceptual clarity require that we draw a clear distinction between generalised demands for greater social equity and an insistence on racial redress.[42]

It is clear that race-based redress and race-based measurement of change receive a large degree of social support, with the obvious corollary that differently raced respondents respond differently. Survey results based on the Reconciliation Barometer show this clearly.[43] Not surprisingly, given the correlation between race and living standards, poorer people indicate much higher levels of support for retaining race in redress than the richest categories.[44] However, poorer people also show widespread dissatisfaction with service delivery at a local level, where their expectations of government are high and they feel badly let down by the failure to improve their living conditions. While race is the explanation for these poor conditions offered by the state, people's daily experience casts a different light on the causes of deprivation. The Reconciliation Barometer's summary of findings during 2013 reflects change and greater attention by respondents and analysts to the articulation of class and race. The executive summary states:

> Key findings show that South Africans regard class to be the single biggest source of division, and the greatest impediment to reconciliation. Race relations, on the other hand, are seen to have improved since 1994, and race has shifted down to the 4th spot on the list of primary sources of division as rated by South Africans. However, further analysis demonstrates that in terms of the racial make-up of material exclusion, race and class remain intimately connected. It is therefore necessary to think more deeply about the nature of the relationship between these two sources of division.[45]

As the survey of attitude studies by Friedman and Erasmus indicate, there exists agreement that 'white people's opinion to racial redress is hostile', to the extent of seeing affirmative action as 'racist'.[46] 'There is not much evidence of a fully developed white consciousness', where such an elite accepts the interdependence of groups, acknowledges responsibility for poor people, and 'develops a belief that efficacious means of assisting the poor exist or might be created'.[47] The hostility, some studies indicate, is reduced when redress is put in terms other than race. Friedman and Erasmus conclude that, as there is an indication that white people see class as more important than race divisions, this 'suggests an awareness of social inequality which could translate into a greater propensity to pay for redress than questions solely based on "race" suggest'. They add, however, that 'this strategy will not work in cases where redress is more about racialised inequalities and less about the intersection of "race" and class inequality'.[48]

My personal experience supports this argument. My parents were well aware of the 'poor white problem', issues of white families having to leave farms and urbanise in the first half of the twentieth century. My mother, for example, made donations on a monthly basis to a wide range of social welfare bodies, most linked to the church, as I discovered when dealing with such affairs at her death. The first Carnegie-funded inquiry into exactly that 'poor white problem' in the 1920s acknowledged the issue. Afrikaner nationalist mobilisation placed great stress on civic responsibility, even if aimed in the first instance at those poor members of their own race. Religion had the potential to extend that responsibility to all, even if it meant a multiracialised all. The overlap between social responsibility and religion would need to be factored into such a strategy of presenting social inequality as a problem of class, or of humane concern, rather than race.

The debate now turns to a critique of capitalism, or at least of present, historically created and local forms of the system. Such a proper debate lies beyond my focus here, even if one agrees that it is essential to an understanding of social problems and to finding ways to address them. The point made by John Holloway applies as much to capitalism as it does to racialism, namely that 'we have created a world which appears to be totally beyond our control, but which in reality depends on our act of constant re-creation'.[49] Capitalism seems to be a 'fact of life', despite the gross injustices it inflicts on people and the environment; despite the global corruption in the banking system; despite the collusive corruption in the construction industry at the time of the soccer World Cup.

In the South African context there are at least two additional points to be made. In the first instance, capitalism is presented in public discourse largely, and deliberately, as consumerism rather than in relation to the sites of production of these consumer goods. This would involve acknowledging exploitation, unemployment, oppressive working conditions, manipulation of 'demand' and so on. The debate, when it occurs, is about where individuals can and should participate in the present utopia, the impossible and immoral utopia of living for what *you* want rather than what *all* need, for the 'more than enough' rather than on how we can ensure enough for everyone.

Paul Gilroy makes the point that after the abolition of slavery, the freedom capitalism afforded former slaves was 'the freedom to consume ... by way of distraction from and compensation for a wider inequality'.[50] Post-1994 South Africa missed an opportunity that has been granted to few societies in this day and age, to learn from the experience of so many other countries, especially those moving beyond colonialism in the late 1950s and 1960s. These lessons were not heeded, nor even explored seriously and radically. Maybe here, too, the belief in South Africa's 'exceptionalism' played a part in the blinkering of the imagination. In a short piece on Nelson Mandela, J.M. Coetzee introduces comments largely absent from discussion of the past:

By the time he became president in his own right, he was already an old man. His failure to throw himself more energetically into the urgent business of the day – the creation of a just economic order – was understandable if unfortunate. Like the rest of the leadership of the ANC, he was blindsided by the collapse of socialism worldwide; the party had no philosophical resistance to put up against a new, predatory economic rationality.[51]

A 'freedom to consume' became the obvious 'benefit' of the local transition to democracy and its accompanying full membership of the global capitalist system. The decision was made by those already part of this system, and by those who knew that they held the power to become participants – and that they deserved it, for themselves and on behalf of the rest.[52]

The second point to be made here is that racialised capitalism is seen as the way out of what is presented as the predicaments, rather than inevitability, of poverty, inequality and unemployment. The displays of wealth are still seen not as provocative but as enviable and desirable, as spurs to individual efforts to escape the trap of poverty. Unemployment on a mass scale is rationalised as a condition that occurs all over the world. In the US context, Fields and Fields draw attention to the effect of the 'initial designation of Afro-Americans as a race on the basis of their class position', namely that it 'colored all subsequent discussion of inequality, even among white persons. In racial disguise, inequality wears a surface camouflage that makes inequality in its most general form – the form that marks and distorts every aspect of our social and political life – hard to see, harder to discuss, and nearly impossible to tackle.'[53] That 'surface camouflage' is to foreground the statistical correlation between race and inequality – a rich white 'nation' and a poor black 'nation' – and to ignore the ongoing creation of inequality. Fields and Fields conclude with reference to the same consequence of privileging and maintaining race ('racecraft' is the provocative term they use to 'highlight the ability of pre- or non-scientific modes of thought to hijack the minds of the scientifically literate'[54]):

Racecraft operates like a railroad switch, diverting a train from one track to another. It is unlike a railroad switch, however, in that the switchman seldom controls where the train ends up. It may end up on a siding in the middle of nowhere, its passengers stranded. By crowding inequality off the public agenda, racecraft has stranded this country [the US] again and again over its history... Forestalling that calamity is our duty. The first and fundamental step in that direction is to observe racecraft in action, study its moves, listen to its language, and root it out. Only after doing so will we be prepared for the still harder work of tackling inequality. Are we up to it?[55]

This is not to argue that race and racism, cultural differentiation, and even religion in some cases have nothing to do with inequality. They can all serve as the basis for discrimination – but this is not systemic as the operation of capitalism is. Anne Phillips draws attention to this wider dimension of inequality, and notes that 'material inequality ... continues to have a recognisable group quality'.[56] It is, however, the meaning we attribute to that 'group quality' that should remain under permanent critical scrutiny.[57]

Earlier in this book I wrote that capitalism as a system knows no colour. That obvious truth does not mean that capitalism cannot adapt to and benefit from the differentials in power relations in societies, including those that accompany race and gender. It does not mean that race and gender cannot be factored into state policies to ensure the most profitably efficient operation of the system – look no further than the apartheid migrant labour system with its articulation of enormously gendered, discriminatory 'traditional' social systems and capitalist production.

To conclude this brief reflection: even if it is near-impossible to imagine a socio-economic system beyond capitalism, and to convince most others of the feasibility of such a world, it is possible to call capitalism to account in other ways of expressing an ideal. Such accounting, if enforced, will indeed create something very different. Two influential thinkers to whom I have referred come to mind here – Zygmunt Bauman and Göran Therborn, in their graphically titled books *Collateral Damage* and *The Killing Fields of Inequality*, respectively.[58] Bauman states his argument as follows: 'There is a selective affinity between social inequality and the likelihood of becoming a casualty of catastrophes, whether man-made or "natural", though in both cases the damage is claimed to be unintended and unplanned.' He writes, in an understatement, that 'it's dangerous to be poor'.[59]

Therborn starts his book with an assessment very similar to the way in which Bauman ends his: 'Inequality is a violation of human dignity; it is a denial of the possibility for everybody's human capabilities to develop … Inequality, then, is not just about the size of wallets. It is a socio-cultural order, which (for most of us) reduces our capabilities to function as human beings.'[60] His book is then how to theorise and evaluate, with descriptions of the world in which we live, the denial of human capabilities brought about by various forces. He argues for three 'dimensions of human capability', with human life seen as 'organisms', which means 'pain, suffering and death'; 'persons', which means 'selves, living their lives in social contexts of meaning and emotion'; and 'actors', in other words 'capable of acting towards aims and goals'.[61] This approach leads him to three 'kinds of inequality', namely 'vital inequality', measured against health and mortality; 'existential inequality', assessed by looking at issues of dignity, rights to respect, and so on; and 'resource inequality', where he adds that 'while the central importance of resource inequality is undeniable', it is not sufficient to start and end here.[62] It is impossible here to fully present his approach and the evidence he provides, but it is enough to suggest that his approach be tested in the South African context, the racialised context.

REFLECTION: FROM SPECIMENS TO SUBJECTS

My concern, throughout this book, is to open debate on what happens when we accept the definition of human beings as specimens of categories, when we have simplified our perspectives on the world to such an extent that the other becomes one-dimensional. So this 'reflection' is just a final reminder. Zygmunt Bauman highlights the most terrible consequences of such abstraction and categorisation – the Holocaust, and genocides in general. 'Genocide differs from other murders in having a *category* for its object. Only the abstract Jews could be subjected to genocide – the kind of murder oblivious to differences of age, sex, personal quality or character.'[63]

The challenge we face, if we want to move beyond this one-dimensionality, is how to recognise individuals as subjects, as complex, and as human. How do we recognise not only other people but ourselves, too, as changing, as able to change in fundamental ways, as more than the list of features implied by the category?

What happens when we accept, in our thinking and practice, that there are no socially relevant fixed distinctions between groups of human beings; that the distinctions we make are not given at birth, but are of our own making or the result of our own acceptance of what is already given? What do we do when there are no races? Once we have asked these questions, we must then ask what new solutions we need to find to deal with the existence of the correlations, in the material world, of those categories with deprivation and fear. Those correlations are there because of the real discrimination based on race, on the effective articulation between capitalism and racism. How do we work towards a truly equal world where children will, in every way, live better lives than their parents, with the opportunities to realise their human capabilities fully?

REFLECTION: THERE ARE NO ENEMIES OVER THE HILLS, WE JUST DON'T KNOW IT

To respond adequately to the challenge of describing the world without resorting to racialism is not easy, but it is a challenge that needs to be met also in the research we do, to give content to calls for social justice. As Kira Erwin writes, in a perceptive reflection on her own research and the use of race categories,

> the lesson … is carefully to think about how our present actions may create checkboxes for our future. If race mattered in the past, and matters now, how do we wish it to matter going forward? Exercises in imagining the future are part utopian thinking and part social engineering. This 'imagineering' demands reflexive research on race by scientists who are mindful of the possible future consequences of such categories.[64]

Erwin accepts Neville Alexander's point that in view of the overlap between 'race' and 'class' there are numerous primary indicators that can be employed in policy formulation and serve as indicators of success or failure of measures to address them, much better than the crudity and harm of race classification.[65] In addition she refers to Alexander's argument that 'social identities seem to have primordial validity for most individuals, precisely because they are not aware of the historical, social

171

and political ways in which their identities have been constructed',[66] and then continues:

> If we agree with this, then research into race can be a consciousness-raising exercise, at least for the researchers, but perhaps also for participants and the wider public. Research that looks at how and why race is constructed in specific ways within a research location – rather than taking perceived racial difference between participants, and between researcher and participants, as givens – offers possibilities for revealing what lies behind the agendas of racialised thought and action.[67]

Here Crain Soudien's call for agency, even an awareness of individual agency, becomes relevant: 'we do not only live in a world which is determined for us by the forces of dominance. We always retain the power, by virtue of being human, to intervene in the processes which seek to determine our fates. Our agency – our will to act – will always carry a value, small or great, in shaping what becomes of us.' Here researchers and activists, and those with whom they interact, can jointly participate in the project of imagining goals beyond the existing limits, towards which to work (what we call utopian thinking). Soudien captures the constricting effect of common sense as follows: 'Imagination and reasoning have the social structure of their contexts imprinted on them.'[68] This social structure is what I have previously referred to as the world into which we are born. As Neuman says, 'we tend to treat our own way of life as natural or normal', we tend to operate within the given. The response required of the researcher, and, in fact, applicable to every thinking, questioning, participating citizen, is 'an attitude of strangeness' or 'questioning and noticing ordinary details or looking at the ordinary through the eyes of a stranger ... It helps him or her see the ordinary in a new way, one that reveals aspects of the setting of which members are not consciously aware.'[69]

Creating a new vocabulary also means rejecting the old, when it is actually a hindrance to creative thinking, and challenging the intellectual imagination. Robert Miles warns against the way in which words associated with 'race', such as 'race relations', become the *explanans* (explanation or explication) for social issues. (We could easily add 'multiracialism', 'diversity', 'multiculturalism' in the South African context). 'Most writers ... deny that they are using the idea of "race" as if it referred to a biological hierarchy of fundamentally different groups of people who possess a variable capacity for "civilisation". Nevertheless, the manner of their use of the notion commonly implies an acceptance of the existence of biological differences between human beings, differences which express the existence of distinct, self-reproducing groups.'[70] My approach is filled with 'what if' questions, deliberately to explore, to see where they take us if we discard, even if just for the moment, the limits set by acceptance of race as a given, the limits to our thinking and to our sense of our own agency.

However, the responsibility for critical thinking lies not only with social scientists, but also with intellectuals in general, with all of us in our capacities of reflection on the world in which we live. Does South Africa welcome such critical thinking? It is worth detouring for a moment through another related matter of concern, namely the devaluation of and attacks on intellectuals in this country – not on all intellectuals, and not consistently, but enough to generate unease. Perhaps it can be taken as evidence of shared concern about this phenomenon that three articles appeared on the same day in the same newspaper, referring to the absence of or the need for critical intellectuals in contemporary South African society.[71] Critical thinking, from all sources, should be valued, not suppressed.

REFLECTION: RACE LABELS DISEMPOWER

Labelling, stereotyping and their effects on self-perceptions can have devastating social consequences. Expectations attached to labels of categories can influence behaviour and performance. This is what Black Consciousness in South Africa at the start aimed at overcoming – reinstating a sense of worth, demanding agency, confirming ability and responsibility.

Nina Jablonski alerted me to the disempowering consequences of such labelling practices when she wrote: 'Human suggestibility thus extends to self-actualization of stereotypes about one's own group.'[72] That can, of course, be both positive, leading to the arrogance of a sense of superiority, and negative, disabling the individual members of oppressed groups. She added: 'Fortunately, the adverse effects of stereotype threat ... can be reduced if a strongly positive and overtly successful role model buffers the negative effects of racial stereotypes.' I would suggest, though, that group-based role models can carry negative values as easily as positive ones. We must be able to question the roles being modelled, no matter how difficult it is to introduce critical perspectives into a context where such roles are being celebrated uncritically.

I referred earlier to Appiah's dismissal of one of the reasons advanced for the retention of race, namely the political solidarity it provides, particularly in response to racism. I have sympathy for a similar argument in South Africa, where support from those 'like me' can be valuable in the face of racist behaviour and attitudes. But one can easily find examples of such group solidarities located elsewhere than in race: for example, in religion and ethnicity, although both of these offer multiple cases where gross violence has been committed in their name. Probably the best answer lies in shared commitments to worthwhile goals such as environmentalism, social justice, or other forms of social activism. But – and this is a very large 'but' – those associations should be voluntary. You choose to live your life in a particular way. You can choose to affiliate with a group with which you want to identify, and you have the freedom to exit from the group. Race classification, on the other hand, does not grant that choice and freedom to individuals. It is ironic that the ANC still decries tribal allegiances, still refers to its own origins in terms of its rejection of the 'divide and rule' acceptance of tribes by colonial authorities and later by apartheid ideologues. And yet it has maintained tribal labels, structures, authority and values, sanctioning them as 'traditional' and therefore beyond criticism, with limited opportunities for exit. Labels can be turned to any purpose by those in power.

REFLECTION: RACE IS ONLY ONE POSSIBLE STORY

It is not just that non-racialism asks for the denial of the deep relevance of categories but that racism demands racialism – race thinking. To address race thinking is to address racism, but in a longer-term fashion than the need to prosecute blatant instances of racism. It is easier, therefore, to follow the route of conferences and resolutions about combating racism, where applause and approval are guaranteed for what are in effect obvious, shallow resolutions and statements. Of course, racism has to be rooted out and cases of racism, whether individual or social, have to be condemned and punished. But this is not all, and it is certainly not sufficient, in the struggle to rid the world of the scourge.

There are several obstacles that have to be confronted in suggesting alternatives to racialism: these have been the main focus of my analysis in earlier chapters. The first hurdle is the sedimentation of the common sense of race thinking, which lies there like a primordial landscape. The second is the attractiveness of race populism to politicians, offering constituencies to be mobilised defensively or aggressively, constituencies that have their origins in the common sense of race. The third is the extreme difficulty of changing the stories of everyday life: social change is characterised by a cultural lag in most societies.[73] Fourth, race thinking and racism serve the interests of the powerful, even if we find that it is easily accepted also by those without power. Fifth, the past is one not only of race thinking, but also of gross abuses of human beings, leaving material scars and also psychological scars, impaired notions of personal ability and group esteem. Any proposed remedy for this damage must address not only grievances, but also grief and its consequences, and internalised notions of worth.

These problems, these obstacles, have been dealt with in some depth in the discussions in this book. The question, then, is how we address these problems through specific projects. My 'reflections' hopefully indicate areas of debate and investigation. But a general approach is worth repeating. As social theorists have proposed, acknowledging and strengthening cross-cutting allegiances and links is a means to weaken the apparent exclusionary fixedness of social identities – like those based on race – that are presented as dominant and even natural in defining social relations.[74] If we can recognise shared interests, shared concerns, shared beliefs, these can contribute to undermining the apparently unquestionable certainties of difference offered by racialism. Competing or at least alternative versions of the constitution of subjects, of stories of everyday life, are available. We need to make deliberate efforts to use these stories as the basis of our social interaction.

If we start off in our everyday lives with the acceptance that race is indeed a social construct, then the manner in which we approach the daily experiences of racism and of race thinking, and of practices and policies based on the easy acceptance of race categories, will be quite different. It will differ from a position that sees race as an essence, a state of being that unavoidably produces attributes of ability (physical, mental, cultural). It will challenge, instead of reinforcing or leaving unexamined, the basis on which we construct identities.

As Fields and Fields say (in relation to the US):

> Racism is a qualitative, not a quantitative, evil. Its harm does not depend on how many people fall under its ban but on the fact that any at all do. And the first principle of racism is belief in race, even if the believer does not deduce from that belief that the member of a race should be enslaved or disenfranchised or shot on sight by trigger-happy police officers or asked for identification when crossing the campus of the university where he teaches, just as believing that the sun travels around the earth is geocentrism, whether or not one deduces from the belief that persons affirming the contrary should be hauled before an inquisition and forced to recant. Once everyone understands that African descent is not race and that African ancestry differs from others only in the racism with which Euro-America has stigmatized it, the problem changes: what is needed is not a more varied set of words and categories to represent racism but a politics to uproot it.[75]

LAST WORDS

It is imperative that science, and especially social science, should return to the processes of and reasons for classification and cast a critical eye over them. Such an approach demands the 'emancipatory' science for which Erik Olin Wright argues,[76] and the curiosity on which the renowned Marxist historian Eric Hobsbawm put such store.[70] Building on an unblinkered critical curiosity, creative thinking has to suggest alternative ways to work towards a society of growing equality in South Africa, without employing the categories, especially of 'race', that were the foundations of apartheid. And this 'utopian thinking' has to be approached with an awareness of the obstacles that exist to dismantling the categories of 'race', and the equally great obstacles to attaining the goal of a society that affords lives of opportunity, dignity and participation to all human beings. François Vourc'h captures this concern as follows:

one takes cognisance of how difficult it is when embarking on a process of deracialisation to do away with the illegitimate categories of apartheid. Who are we if we are no longer blacks, coloureds or whites? It is neither simple nor evident how to implement a policy that wipes clean the slate of racist ties without affording the victims of this odious system the opportunity to be vindicated for their oppression and to gain recognition for the extreme prejudice endured in an all too recent past. 'Yes' to deracialising social relations and ties, but for whose benefit?[78]

I accept the case Vourc'h makes, and would answer the concluding question thus: For the benefit of all, but in ways that are also differently implemented to meet specific needs. To remain enthralled by the common sense of racialism diminishes all of us in the long run. Escaping from it becomes more and more difficult. The most suitable revenge we can take on the racist past of apartheid is to work towards a society beyond and without race. We need to see the achievement of equality based on non-racialism as the revolutionary task of all South Africans.

Thus far, instead of forging a new society in post-1994 South Africa we have given further evidence for what, in the context of the US, Judith Butler described as *'the historical time that we thought was past [and which] turns out to structure the contemporary field with a persistence that gives the lie to history as chronology'*.[79] This is the legacy of the present that we carry with us, even as we commit ourselves to a utopia of our own imagining.

I will end with Michael Root's concluding words: 'Laws of nature do not make race real, we do. While the social sciences can explain how or why we so divide ourselves, we need to decide whether we ought to.'[80] It is a complex but essential task.

Notes

Newspaper abbreviations

BD	*Business Day* [national daily]
CA	*Cape Argus* [Cape Town daily]
CT	*Cape Times* [Cape Town morning daily]
DB	*Die Burger* [Cape Town morning daily – Afrikaans]
DN	*Daily News* [Durban-based]
M	*The Mercury* [Durban morning daily]
M(BR)	*The Mercury (Business Report)* [*Business Report* is a supplement to national morning dailies and *SI* and *STb*]
M&G	*Mail & Guardian* [National weekly]
P	*Post* [KZN-based]
R	*Rapport* [Sunday national – Afrikaans]
RDM	*Rand Daily Mail* [liberal-left daily under apartheid]
SI	*Sunday Independent* [Sunday national]
SI(BR)	*Sunday Independent (Business Report)* [see *M(BR)* above]
St	*The Star* [Johannesburg based daily]
ST	*Sunday Times* [Sunday national]
ST(x)	*Sunday Times Extra* ['Indian community' supplement to *ST*]
ST(BT)	*Sunday Times (Business Times)* (supplement to *ST*)
STb(H)	*Sunday Tribune (Herald)* (supplement for the 'Indian community' to Durban-based Sunday paper)
TT	*The Times* [national daily – linked to *ST*]
TW	*The Witness* [Pietermaritzburg-based daily]
WW	*Weekend Witness* [Saturday edition of *The Witness*]

Dedication

1 Kathryn Mills and Pamela Mills (eds.), *C. Wright Mills: Letters and autobiographical writing* (Berkeley, CA: University of California Press, 2000).

Introduction

1 Lawrence A. Hirschfeld, *Race in the Making: Cognition, culture, and the child's construction of human kinds* (Cambridge, MA.: MIT Press, 1996), p. x.
2 Michael Billig, *Banal Nationalism* (London: Sage, 1995), p. 8.
3 Shaun Johnson, *The Native Commissioner* (Johannesburg: Penguin, 2006).
4 Dan O'Meara, *Volkskapitalisme: Class, capital and ideology in the development of Afrikaner nationalism 1934–1948* (Johannesburg: Ravan Press, 1983), p. 38.
5 Hannes Haasbroek, *'n Seun soos Bram: 'n Portret van Bram Fischer en sy ma Ella* (Cape Town: Umuzi, 2011), pp. 121–2.
6 Haasbroek, *Seun soos Bram*, p. 200.
7 Glenn Moss, *The New Radicals: A generational memoir of the 1970s* (Auckland Park: Jacana, 2014).
8 Judy Connors, 'An evaluative history of the South African Conscientious Objectors Support Group (COSG): Nonviolent resistance to conscription and the militarization of the apartheid regime' (Unpublished MComm thesis (Conflict Resolution and Peace Studies), University of KwaZulu-Natal, 2008).
9 See Billy Keniston, *Choosing to Be Free: The life story of Rick Turner* (Johannesburg: Jacana, 2013), pp. 95–6.
10 Rick Turner, *The Eye of the Needle: An essay on participatory democracy* (Johannesburg: Special Programme for Christian Action in Society, 1972; republished with a biographical introduction by Tony Morphet, by Ravan Press, 1980). Online: http://www.scribd.com/doc/55744023/The-Eye-of-the-Needle-by-Richard-Turner.
11 For some information on the trial of the Afrikaans poet and artist Breyten Breytenbach, charged under the Terrorism Act, alternatively the Suppression of Communism Act, see SAIRR (South African Institute of Race Relations), *A Survey of Race Relations in South Africa 1975* (Johannesburg: SAIRR, 1976), pp. 63–5, and SAIRR, *A Survey of Race Relations in South Africa 1976* (Johannesburg: SAIRR, 1977), p. 127. Also see Moss, *New Radicals*, chapter 9.
12 SAIRR (South African Institute of Race Relations), *A Survey of Race Relations in South Africa 1966* (Johannesburg: SAIRR, 1967), pp. 1–7.
13 See, for example, Gerhard Maré and Georgina Hamilton, *An Appetite for Power: Buthelezi's Inkatha and South Africa* (Johannesburg: Ravan Press; Bloomington and Indianapolis: Indiana University Press, 1987), and Gerhard Maré, *Brothers Born of Warrior Blood: Politics and ethnicity in South Africa* (Johannesburg: Ravan Press, 1992; London and New York: Zed (as *Ethnicity and Politics in South Africa* (1993)).
14 Race, as it operates in race thinking, is not simply a neutral descriptor of appearance. I will not distract the reader by employing quotation marks repeatedly to make this point, except when I wish to indicate that I am discussing the concept, the idea, the notion of 'race', or where I quote others who have used the term. And I will certainly try to indicate what I think other people mean when they speak of race or an alternative term (such as 'population group', 'ethnic group', 'cultural group', 'nation', etc), especially when interpretation is important and necessary. For the same reason, I will, without unnecessary comment, use the terms that were employed under apartheid and that continue to be employed, such as Coloured, Indian, white and black.

Chapter 1

1 Brian Fay, *Contemporary Philosophy of Social Science* (Oxford: Blackwell, 1999), p. 73, emphasis added.

2 Neville Alexander, 'Affirmative action and the perpetuation of racial identities in post-apartheid South Africa', *Transformation* 63 (2007), p. 93.

3 Robert Miles, *Racism* (London: Routledge, 1989), pp. 69–73.

4 Miles, *Racism*, p. 71.

5 Kwame Anthony Appiah, *In My Father's House: Africa in the philosophy of culture* (Oxford: Oxford University Press, 1992), p. 13.

6 Alexander, 'Affirmative action', p. 93.

7 'Race is a social construct' can, however, become a slogan rather than an approach in arguing against racialism. For such an argument, see Eric C. Thompson, 'The problem of "race as a Social Construct"', *Anthropology News*, November (2006), p. 6.

8 Fay, *Contemporary Philosophy*, p. 74.

9 Zygmunt Bauman, *Modernity and the Holocaust* (Ithaca, NY: Cornell University Press, 2000), p. 227.

10 Martha Lampland and Susan Leigh Star, 'Reckoning with standards', in Martha Lampland and Susan Leigh Star (eds.), *Standards and Their Stories: How quantifying, classifying, and formalizing practices shape everyday life* (Ithaca, NY: Cornell University Press, 2009).

11 Bauman, *Modernity*, p. 227, emphases original.

12 Violent protests broke in Sibongile township, in northern KwaZulu-Natal in May 2013, to do with the suspension of the municipal manager. Non-South African shop keepers were on the receiving end of looting and physical attacks (http://www.iol. co.za/dailynews/news/violence-breaks-out-in-dundee-1.1513591).

13 Alexander, 'Affirmative action', p. 93.

14 Melissa Nobles, *Shades of Citizenship: Race and the census in modern politics* (Stanford, CA: Stanford University Press, 2000), p. 180.

15 Richard Jenkins, *Social Identity* (London: Routledge, 1996), p. 128.

16 Michael Billig, *Banal Nationalism* (London: Sage, 1995), p. 8.

17 Billig, *Banal Nationalism*, p. 93.

18 Yvonne Erasmus, 'Racial (re)classification during apartheid South Africa:Regulations, experiences and the meaning(s) of "race"' (Unpublished PhD thesis, St George's, University of London, 2007), p. 83.

19 Erasmus, 'Racial (re)classification', p. 3.

20 SAIRR (South African Institute of Race Relations), *A Survey of Race Relations in South Africa 1969* (Johannesburg: SAIRR, 1970), pp. 23–4.

21 SAIRR, *Survey of Race Relations 1969*, pp. 24–5.

22 Erasmus, 'Racial (re)classification', p. 101.

23 Erasmus, 'Racial (re)classification', p. 102.

24 Erasmus, 'Racial (re)classification', pp. 229–30.

25 Erasmus, 'Racial (re)classification', p. 101.

26 Erasmus, 'Racial (re)classification', p. 239.

27 Erasmus, 'Racial (re)classification', p. 236; Kevin Durrheim and John Dixon, 'Everyday explanation of diversity and difference: The role of lay ontologizing', in George Ellison and Alan Goodman (eds.), *The Nature of Difference: Science, society and human biology* (London: Routledge, 2006), for post-1994.

28 Laurine Platzky and Cherryl Walker, *The Surplus People: Forced removals in South Africa* (Johannesburg: Ravan Press, 1985); Mamphela Ramphele, *A Bed Called Home: Life in the migrant labour hostels of Cape Town* (Cape Town: David Philip; Athens, OH: Ohio University Press; Edinburgh: Edinburgh University Press, 1993).

29 Thomas Karis and Gail M. Gerhart (eds.), *From Protest to Challenge: A documentary*

history of African politics in South Africa 1882–1964, Vol. 3 *Challenge to Violence 1953–1964* (Stanford, CA: Hoover Institution Press, 1987), pp. 205–8.

30 Gerhard Maré, '"Non-racialism" in the struggle against apartheid', *Society in Transition* 34, 1 (2003).

31 Rob Davies, Dan O'Meara and Sipho Dlamini, *The Struggle for South Africa: A reference guide to movements, organizations and institutions*, 2 vols. (London: Zed, 1984); Allison Drew (ed.), *South Africa's Radical Tradition: A documentary history*, 2 vols. (Cape Town: Buchu Books, Mayibuye Books, UCT Press, 1996, 1997).

32 Thomas Karis and Gail M. Gerhart (eds.), *From Protest to Challenge: A documentary history of African politics in South Africa 1882–1964*, Vol. 4 *Political Profiles 1882–1964* (Stanford, CA: Hoover Institution Press, 1977), p. 2; Crain Soudien, 'The contribution of radical Western Cape intellectuals to an indigenous knowledge project in South Africa', *Transformation* 76 (2011).

33 Thomas Karis and Gail M. Gerhart (eds.), *From Protest to Challenge: A documentary history of African politics in South Africa 1882–1990*, Vol. 5 *Nadir and Resurgence 1964–1979* (Bloomington and Indianapolis, IN: Indiana University Press, 1997), Chapter 4, pp. 459–62.

34 Xolela Mangcu, *Biko: A biography* (Cape Town: Tafelberg, 2012), pp. 281–2, quoting from Steve Biko, *I Write What I Like* (London: Heinemann 1988), pp. 146–8.

35 *RDM*, 20 June 1964, reprinted in Karis and Gerhart, *From Protest to Challenge*, Vol. 5, pp. 356–8; also see Ryan Brown, *A Native of Nowhere: The life of Nat Nakasa* (Auckland Park: Jacana, 2013).

Prologue to Part Two

1 Walter Benjamin (translated by Howard Eiland and Kevin McLaughlin), *The Arcades Project* (Cambridge, MA: The Belknap Press of Harvard University Press, 1999), pp. 871–2.

2 Quoted in J.M. Coetzee, 'The marvels of Walter Benjamin', *New York Review of Books* (January 2001), p. 32.

3 Benjamin, *Arcades Project*, p. ix.

4 Benjamin, *Arcades Project*, p. x.

5 Benjamin, *Arcades Project*, p. x.

6 Coetzee, 'Marvels of Walter Benjamin', p. 33.

7 Readers are referred to a report by the SA Human Rights Commission into racism in the media. The hearings, commissioned research and the report created extensive debate, critical and supportive. I am, however, dealing here with the vocabulary of race rather than racism. See http://www.sahrc.org.za/home/21/files/Reports/Racism%20 in%20the%20media_%20interim%20report.pdf, accessed July 2013.

8 *TW*, 8 April 2014.

9 *P*, 21–25 November 2012; *DN*, 22 November 2012.

10 Lee Stone and Yvonne Erasmus, 'Race thinking and the law in post-1994 South Africa', *Transformation* 79 (2012), pp. 133–5. Original and full report for the Centre for Critical Research on Race and Identity, University of KwaZulu-Natal (published online 10 November 2008) http://ccrri.ukzn.ac.za/docs/FINAL%20REPORT%20 ON%20RACE%20THINKING%2010%20NOVEMBER%202008.pdf.

11 Stone and Erasmus, 'Race thinking and the law', pp. 131–3.

12 Stone and Erasmus, 'Race thinking and the law', pp. 135–8.

Chapter 2

1 RSA (Republic of South Africa), Constitution of the Republic of South Africa, No 108

of 1996 (Cape Town: Office of the President, 1996).

2 In defence of his State of the Nation' address, President Jacob Zuma described 'economic freedom' as resting on 'deracialising' ownership, management and control of the economy (*TT*, 21 February 2014).

3 See, for example, the Presidential State of the Nation address of 14 February 2013.

4 http://www.southafrica.info/about/people/population.htm#.Uuddnv3g6Wc, accessed 28 January 2014.

5 H. Sonnabend, 'Population', in Ellen Hellmann (ed.), *Handbook on Race Relations in South Africa* (Cape Town: Oxford University Press, 1949), pp. 6, 9. Note that South African population statistics are notoriously difficult to quantify accurately, even more so in the past where numbers were counted differently and where assessment was tainted by the location of black people, in 'Reserves' and 'bantustans', as marginal to the white-dominated and more urbanised core.

6 Göran Therborn, *The Ideology of Power and the Power of Ideology* (London: Verso, 1999).

7 Pierre de Vos, 'Looking backward, looking forward: "Race", corrective measures and the South African Constitutional Court', *Transformation* 79 (2012), p. 161.

8 http://www.dailymaverick.co.za/opinionista/2014-01-23-why-redress-measures-are-not-racist/#.UuePtP3g6Wc, accessed 28 January 2014.

9 Anthony Marx, *Making Race and Nation: A comparison of the United States, South Africa and Brazil* (Cambridge: Cambridge University Press, 1998), p. 267. While Alexander agrees with Marx on this point, he qualifies the use he makes of Marx's findings by distancing himself from the 'racial domination' that Marx refers to. Marx's study referred to pre-1994 South Africa where both segregationist and apartheid South Africa represented racial domination, whereas Alexander was writing in a post-1994 context where domination of one race group by another was no longer the political agenda. The general point holds.

10 *R*, 11 October 2009, own translation.

11 Vuyo Jack in *SI(BR)*, 16 September 2007.

12 See Bill Freund, 'Swimming against the tide: The Macro-Economic Research Group in the South African transition 1991–94', *Review of African Political Economy* 40, 138 (2013), p. 530.

13 ANC (African National Congress), 'RDP: The Reconstruction and Development Programme: a policy framework' (1994), <http://www.nelsonmandela.org/omalley/index.php/site/q/03lv02039/04lv02103/05lv02120/06lv02126.htm>, accessed November 2013, pp. 2–3.

14 ANC, 'RDP', p. 3.

15 ANC, 'RDP', p. 47.

16 ANC, 'RDP', section 1.3.4, p. 6.

17 ANC, 'RDP', p. 61.

18 ANC, 'RDP', p. 81.

19 ANC, 'RDP', p. 82.

20 ANC, 'RDP', section 4.8.13, p. 75.

21 On GEAR see, for example, Vishnu Padayachee, 'The South African economy, 1994–2004', *Social Research* 72, 3 (2005).

22 *M&G*, 8–14 February 2013.

23 http://www.news24.com/SouthAfrica/Politics/ANC-has-abandoned-the-Freedom-Charter-Numsa-20131220, accessed February 2014.

24 http://www.news24.com/SouthAfrica/Politics/ANC-remembers-Freedom-Charter-20130626, accessed February 2014.

25 http://www.news24.com/MyNews24/Clever-blacks-for-ANC-20130805, accessed December 2013.

Chapter 3

1 Bill Freund, 'Swimming against the tide: The Macro-Economic Research Group in the South African transition 1991–94', *Review of African Political Economy* 40, 138 (2013), p. 532.

2 See, for example, Muriel Horrell, *Laws Affecting Race Relations in South Africa* (Johannesburg: SAIRR, 1978), pp. 6–8.

3 Sheila van der Horst, 'Labour', in Ellen Hellmann (ed.), *Handbook on Race Relations in South Africa* (Cape Town: Oxford University Press, 1949), p. 109.

4 Dan O'Meara, *Forty Lost Years: The apartheid state and the politics of the National Party, 1948–1994* (Johannesburg: Ravan Press; Athens, OH: Ohio University Press, 1996), p. 61.

5 Benjamin Roberts, Gina Weir-Smith and Vasu Reddy, 'Minding the gap: Attitudes toward affirmative action in South Africa', *Transformation* 77 (2011), p. 13.

6 Lee Stone and Yvonne Erasmus, 'Race thinking and the law in post-1994 South Africa', *Transformation* 79 (2012), p. 133. Original and full report for the Centre for Critical Research on Race and Identity, University of KwaZulu-Natal (published online 10 November 2008) <http://ccrri.ukzn.ac.za/docs/FINAL%20REPORT%20 ON%20RACE%20THINKING%2010%20NOVEMBER%202008.pdf>.

7 *ST*, 19 September 1995.

8 Heinz Klug, 'Participating in the design: Constitution-making in South Africa', in Penelope Andrews and Stephen Ellmann (eds.), *The Post-Apartheid Constitutions: Perspectives on South Africa's basic law* (Johannesburg: Witwatersrand University Press; Athens, OH: Ohio University Press, 2001), p. 140.

9 The term 'generic black' is to capture the combination of 'black, Indian and 'Coloured' as the collective 'designated group' 'black' in the EEA. The University of Stellenbosch tracks race-based transformation by using the acronym 'BSI' (Bruin, Swart, Indiër or Brown, Black, Indian).

10 Ivor Chipkin, 'Transcending bureaucracy: State transformation in the age of the manager', *Transformation* 77 (2011), p. 47.

11 Vinothan Naidoo, 'Assessing racial redress in the civil service', in Adam Habib and Kristina Bentley (eds.), *Racial Redress and Citizenship in South Africa* (Cape Town: HSRC Press, 2008), p. 125.

12 Such as by Adam Habib and Kristina Bentley, 'An alternative framework for redress and citizenship', in Adam Habib and Kristina Bentley (eds.), *Racial Redress and Citizenship in South Africa* pp. 342–4.

13 SAIRR (South African Institute of Race Relations), *Fast Facts* 7/97, also reported on in *R*, 20 July 1997. My thanks to Lerato Moloi of the SAIRR, who helped me find copies of *Fast Facts*.

14 *Fast Facts* 7/97, also 11/96.

15 Stone and Erasmus, 'Race thinking and the law', pp. 133–4, list legislation 'allowing/ facilitating [fair] discrimination on the basis of race': Public Services Act (1994), Skills Development Act (1998), Employment Equity Act (1998) and the Broad-Based Black Economic Empowerment Act (2003). Stone and Erasmus also mention that 'other industry based legislation makes black economic empowerment objectives one of the criteria for obtaining licences, rights and so forth, for example the 1998 Marine Living Resources Act and the 2002 Mineral and Petroleum Resources Development Act'. In terms of facilitation, we could add the Constitution (1996) and the Promotion of Equality and Prevention of Unfair Discrimination Act (2000).

16 For discussion of the legal arguments made to support such a position see, for example, Stone and Erasmus, 'Race thinking and the law', p. 125, and Pierre de Vos, 'Looking backward, looking forward: "Race", corrective measures and the South African Constitutional Court', *Transformation* 79 (2012).

17 http://www.iol.co.za/news/politics/bee-deals-only-benefit-the-few-1.393711#.
   UvJegP2KjlI, accessed January 2014.
18 http://www.financialmail.co.za/features/2014/03/20/tender-spot-for-civil-servants,
   accessed April 2014.
19 *R*, 23 October 2011, own translation.
20 Sipho Kings in *M&G*, 14–20 March 2014.
21 The directive (reproduced in Laurine Platzky and Cherryl Walker, *The Surplus
   People: Forced removals in South Africa*, p. 24), as is clear from the formulation,
   was actually aimed at further restricting the movement of 'Blacks' rather than
   advancing 'Coloureds' through a 'preferential employment' area, and followed on the
   withdrawal of a bizarrely-named set of bills, one of which was entitled the 'Orderly
   Movement and Settlement of Black Persons Bill', in 1982; also Platzky and Walker,
   Surplus People, p. 23, and Ian Goldin, *Making Race: The politics and economics of
   coloured identity in South Africa* (London: Longman, 1987).
22 Platzky and Walker, *Surplus People*, p. 24, for a formal letter spelling out of the
   policy.
23 Platzky and Walker, *Surplus People*, p. 395.
24 See https://www.youtube.com/watch?v=oBqCD_498hY. Jimmy Manyi has been a
   familiar figure on the conference and workshop circuit for several years, an ambitious,
   eloquent, confrontational and very confident speaker (http://whoswho.co.za/jimmy-
   manyi-5143). He has been president of the Black Management Forum, and at the same
   time has served variously as director-general in the national Department of Labour,
   spokesperson for the Presidency, head of the government's communication unit, and
   head of the Commission for Employment Equity. In the private sector, Manyi has
   served in human resources positions in large corporations such as Tiger Brands, IBM
   and Barclays Bank plc, and in banking and marketing at Nedcor Peoples Bank (see,
   for example, *ST(BT)*, 27 September 2009). In 2013 he was reported to be 'driving
   the creation of the Progressive Professional Forum, which he hopes will give better
   qualified card-carrying members of the ANC more of a voice in the party' (*ST(BT)*, 28
   April 2013, also *SI*, 5 May 2013).
25 Platzky and Walker, *Surplus People*.
26 See Trevor Manuel, for example: http://www.iol.co.za/news/politics/trevor-manuel-s-
   open-letter-to-jimmy-manyi-1.1034606#.Ui91C1WSySo, accessed April 2014.
27 *M*, 25 July 2000.
28 *DN*, 5 February 2004.
29 See http://www.dhet.gov.za/LinkClick.aspx?fileticket=18oxu4C%2F%2FUA%3D&
   tabid=92&mid=495, p28, accessed April 2014; for pre-2014 university approaches
   see, for example, http://www.timeshighereducation.co.uk/news/sa-quotas-to-favour-
   black-medics/107614.article, and http://www.politicsweb.co.za/politicsweb/view/
   politicsweb/en/page71616/page71656?oid=86906&sn=Detail, accessed April 2014,
   1998 and 2007 respectively.
30 See http://www.highbeam.com/doc/1G1-366931364.html.
31 Zimitri Erasmus, 'Confronting the categories: Equitable admission without apartheid
   race classification', *South African Journal of Higher Education* 24, 2 (2010); also
   recent debates in the media on medical schools, especially at the universities of
   Cape Town and the Witwatersrand – Xolela Mangcu (*CT*, 20 February 2013 and
   27 February 2013); Max Price (*ST*, 24 November 2013); and Adam Habib (*ST*, 2
   February 2014).
32 *CT*, 12 September 2012.
33 The racialised subdivisions of 'generic black' create awkward political ramifications.
   The ANC secretary-general, Gwede Mantashe, had to make the absurd claim (after
   'meeting with coloured leaders') that 'it was a "mistake" that coloured people

considered themselves a minority. "You can't be part of a majority [black], and then define yourself as a minority"' (*TT*, 11 November 2013). Earlier, the columnist Thebe Mabanga complained that Coloureds wanted best of two worlds – white and black – and by 'continuing to play the part of an oppressed minority, some coloureds are hoping to secure some kind of special status in empowerment programmes' (*ST(BT)*, 13 May 2007).

34 http://www.iol.co.za/news/politics/ben-turok-s-letter-to-manyi-1.1043633#. Uw3Xgv2KhFI, accessed February 2014. A strong exception, but Trevor Manuel, an ANC minister, also took issue through an open letter: http://www.iol.co.za/news/politics/trevor-manuel-s-open-letter-to-jimmy-manyi-1.1034606#.U3zg_MY5v1o, accessed April 2014.

35 *CT*, 27 August 2012.

36 *TT*, 17 May 2012.

37 See, for example, interview in *ST*, 19 May 2013.

38 Southern African Legal Information Institute, http://www.saflii.org.za/za/cases/ZALCCT/2013/38.html, accessed February 2014.

39 See Ian Hacking, *The Social Construction of What?* (Cambridge, MA: Harvard University Press, 1999).

40 Neville Alexander, *Thoughts on the New South Africa* (Auckland Park: Jacana, 2013), pp. 166–71.

41 Alexander, *Thoughts on the New South Africa*, p. 168.

42 Yoon Jung Park, 'Black, yellow, (honorary) white or just plain South African: Chinese South Africans, identity and affirmative action', *Transformation* 77 (2011), p. 128, note 12; Heribert Adam and Kogila Moodley, 'Diversity management in Canada', in Wilmot James, Daria Caliguire and Kerry Cullinan (eds.), *Now That We Are Free: Coloured communities in a democratic South Africa* (Cape Town: IDASA, 1996), pp. 110–17.

43 See also Gerhard Maré, '"Fear of numbers": Reflections on the South African case', *Current Sociology* 59, 5 (2011).

44 The Constitution of the post-1994 Republic of South Africa recognises 'kings', 'traditional authority' and 'traditional areas' with rules of behaviour and legal practice specific to them.

45 John Comaroff and Jean Comaroff, *Ethnicity, Inc.* (Scottsville: University of KwaZulu-Natal Press; Chicago: University of Chicago Press, 2009).

46 In 2014, new 'draft regulations to the EEA were gazetted and drew renewed criticism of the Act and its implementation. It came in for criticism even from ANC provincial leaders in the Western Cape – not surprisingly just before elections in May. For example, it confirmed and gave detailed instructions on the use of 'national demographics' in top employment levels, with a mix of national and regional in the next level down 'technical, semi-skilled and unskilled in all companies employing more than 150 people', writes Lynley Donnelly (*M&G*, 28 March – 3 April 2014).

47 *BD*, 4 July 2008. Quotations used by Yvonne Erasmus and Yoon Jung Park, 'Racial classification, redress and citizenship: The case of the Chinese South Africans', *Transformation* 68 (2008).

48 Erasmus and Park, 'Racial classification', pp. 99–100.

49 Erasmus and Park, 'Racial classification', p. 101.

50 Park, 'Black, yellow, (honorary) white', p. 118.

51 In his column 'Black Jack', *SI(BR)*, 13 August 2006.

52 Arjun Appadurai, *Fear of Small Numbers: An essay on the geography of anger* (Durham, NC: Duke University Press, 2006), p. 83, emphases original.

53 *M*, 15 May 2007.

54 *R*, 9 September 2007.

55 *ST*, 9 September 2007.
56 *ST(BT)*, 16 September 2007.
57 *M(BR)*, 24 October 2008.
58 *TT*, 30 June 2011.
59 *ST(BT)*, 30 June 2013.
60 *TT*, 6 February 2014.

Chapter 4

1 SAIRR (South African Institute of Race Relations), *Race Relations Survey 1986* (Johannesburg: SAIRR, 1977), pp. 338-9.
2 Botha quoted in S.D. Girvin, 'Race and race classification', in A.J. Rycroft, L.J. Boulle, M.K. Robertson and P.R. Spiller (eds.), *Race and the Law in South Africa* (Cape Town: Juta, 1987), p. 5, emphases added.
3 SAIRR, *Survey of Race Relations 1986*, p. 338.
4 SAIRR, *Survey of Race Relations 1986*, p. 339.
5 SAIRR (South African Institute of Race Relations), *Race Relations Survey 1991/2* (Johannesburg: SAIRR, 1992), p. 1.
6 SAIRR, *Survey of Race Relations 1991/2*, p. 457.
7 I was not able to establish whether such a document is still in use, or if it is used in other municipalities.
8 Deborah Posel, 'What's in a name? Race categorisations under apartheid and their afterlife', *Transformation* 47 (2001), p. 57.
9 http://www.labourguide.co.za/employment-equity/756-why-employers-cannot-ignore-equity-laws, accessed January 2014.
10 *WW*, 28 November 2009.
11 Chris Saunders, 'The future of Natal/KwaZulu: The pursuit of non-racial capitalism'. Opening address to the USSALEP conference on 'Development for Employment' held at Amanzimnyama Hill, Tongaat, Natal on Friday, 4 November 1983.
12 See, for example, KwaZulu-Natal Indaba in Gerhard Maré and Georgina Hamilton, *An Appetite for Power: Buthelezi's Inkatha and South Africa* (Johannesburg: Ravan Press; Bloomington and Indianapolis: Indiana University Press, 1987).
13 Saunders, 'Future of Natal/KwaZulu', p. 7.
14 Saunders, 'Future of Natal/KwaZulu', p. 4.
15 Saunders, 'Future of Natal/KwaZulu', p. 12.
16 See online at http://www.armsdeal-vpo.co.za/articles03/temptation.html, accessed February 2014; and *CA*, 12 March 2003.
17 *M*, 22 November 1999.
18 Hein Marais, *South Africa Pushed to the Limit: The political economy of change* (Cape Town: UCT Press, 2011), p. 140.
19 Marais, *South Africa Pushed to the Limit*, p. 141.
20 Marais, *South Africa Pushed to the Limit*, p. 142.
21 See Sampie Terreblanche, *A History of Inequality in South Africa 1652–2002* (Scottsville: University of Natal Press; Sandton: CMM Review, 2002), p. 33, Table 2.2 for changing inequality of income, also pp. 441–4.
22 *M(BR)*, 21 July 2011. Cronin was quoted from the SACP journal *Umsebenzi* 10, 15 (http://www.sacp.org.za/main.php?ID=3436), where he writes: 'A fixation on the colour or gender of the agents and individual capitalists involved in monopoly capital can easily delude us into imagining that changing people will change monopoly capital. Surely more than a decade of experience has taught us that it is the boardroom that changes the person, and not the person the boardroom. Of course we are not arguing that boardrooms or share-ownership should be reserved for white males. Nor are we

denying that some capitalists might be reasonably decent human beings as individuals, while others are just awful. But we are reminding ourselves of what cde Chris Hani expressed so succinctly: "the point is not to transfer power [from some individuals to others], but to TRANSFORM it." For any consistent Marxist the problem with monopoly capital in SA is not that it is white, but that it is concentrated capital locked into the universal laws of capitalist reproduction and exploitation regardless of who is in the boardroom. ... While populist demagogues might scream about "imperialism" and "monopoly capital" – the threats to carry out nationalization and expropriation simply increase (as they are meant to) the length of the queues of wealthy supplicants outside their office doors, the numbers of sponsorships, the gifts of whisky and helicopter trips they are offered from the very monopoly capital they are threatening!' For a fascinating evaluation of the SACP's participation, through the ANC's BEE policy, in deracialising capitalism, see CPGB (Communist Party of Great Britain), 'Ideologically bankrupt' in *Weekly Worker* 918 (2012) (http://www.cpgb. org.uk/home/weekly-worker/918/ideologically-bankrupt, accessed 26 May 2013).

23 Reports include: http://www.iol.co.za/business/news/bee-law-makeover-to-rule-out-fronting-1.1588363#.U0bg4ycayK0, http://www.moneyweb.co.za/moneyweb-south-africa/complex-bee-fronting, http://www.citypress.co.za/business/hamon-bust-for-fronting-20121124/, and http://www.citypress.co.za/business/bosasa-faces-dti-fronting-investigation/, accessed April 2014.

24 *M(BR)*, 19 August 2002).

25 Reported *M*, 30 January 2008. It is worth noting that 'verification' (i.e. the 'authentification' of individual membership of 'races') is referred to as an 'industry', just as 'diversity management' had become. This is yet another indication of how race, without which this system would collapse, is being embedded within capitalism itself, not just as beneficiary of exploitation but as a money-making scheme in itself, with its own workforce, removing the messy business of race classification from public acknowledgement and state participation. Brigitte Brun's employer describes itself in the follow terms:

'AQRate Verification Services is a Broad-Based BEE verification brand consisting of 4 private companies with shared ownership, management, verification methodology, commitment to transformation and an ethos of "independent, credible, assurance".

'The brand came to be in June 2009 following an unbundling of shareholding in the National Empowerment Rating Agency (NERA) [a private sector] holding entity which saw two of the then three accredited verification agencies in the NERA group re-brand to AQRate (Pty) Ltd (previously NERA – Western Cape) and AQRate KZN (Pty) Ltd (previously NERA – KZN). The previous NERA office in Limpopo also rebranded to AQRate. AQRate Gauteng commenced business during June 2009.

'As such, an AQRate rating is official recognition that your organisation is in compliance with the Broad Based Black Economic Empowerment Act and the Codes of Good Practice. We are the only verification agency brand that has been accredited to deliver BEE verification services in more than one geographical location in South Africa. Our Cape Town, Kwazulu-Natal and Gauteng offices have been independently accredited by the South African National Accreditation System (SANAS) as part of the very first batch of 11 verification agencies to be accredited in South Africa in February 2009. This national presence affords AQRate the market presence associated with a true market leader and national player' (www.aqrate.co.za/about/, accessed 6 November 2012)

The website even offers 'Africandi – The BEE Calculator App is an innovative, easy-to-user calculator which allows you to establish your B-BBEE score from your phone, tablet or computer'.

'What is SANAS, the SA National Accreditation System? Provides certification (maintaining the "standards" by which to ensure that such practices as Blood Transfusion and BBBEE verification is guaranteed genuine) recognised by the SA government' (home.sanas.co.za/ , accessed January 2014). Once assessed and accredited, the 'verification agency' becomes a member of Abva (the Association of BEE Verification Agencies).

Another company, BEE Empowered, describes their service as: 'Turn BEE Verification to your advantage. In South Africa today, the higher your Black Economic Empowerment score, the more opportunities your business has access to – especially when it comes to tenders. Choose a SANAS-accredited and very experienced BEE Verification Agency that gets to know your business first, then applies a unique blend of business, procurement, legal and labour law expertise to optimise your BEE rating' (online at Bempowered.net, accessed April 2014). What on earth is 'verification methodology' if it does not include race classification and race certification? Of course it does, in terms of a Verification Manual, produced by the Department of Trade and Industries (DTI) and to be found at https://www.thedti.gov.za/economic_ empowerment/bee_veri_manual.jsp.

It is to be expected that BEE verification would become an 'industry', much as 'diversity management' did – a practice also relying on knowing about races and their attributes. In a recent book on 'diversity interventions' diversity management is defined, in the glossary of terms in the following way: 'Managing diversity is different from valuing diversity because it focuses on the business case for diversity. In this scenario, capitalising on diversity is seen as a strategic approach to business that contributes to organisational goals such as profits and productivity'. Any support service that improves 'profit and productivity' can be sold. Melissa Steyn (ed.), *Being Different Together: Case studies on diversity interventions in some South African organisations* (Cape Town: iNCUDISA, University of Cape Town, 2010), p. 12.

26 *M&G*, 27 July 2007.
27 *M*, 9 May 2007.
28 Lee Stone and Yvonne Erasmus, 'Race thinking and the law in post-1994 South Africa', *Transformation* 79 (2012), pp. 135–8.
29 Melissa Nobles, *Shades of Citizenship: Race and the census in modern politics* (Stanford, CA: Stanford University Press, 2000), p. 1.
30 Nobles, *Shades of Citizenship*, p. 11.
31 See, for example, Gerhard Maré, '"Fear of numbers": Reflections on the South African case', *Current Sociology* 59, 5 (2011); Yvonne Erasmus, 'Racial (re)classification during apartheid South Africa: regulations, experiences and the meaning(s) of "race"' (Unpublished PhD thesis, St George's, University of London, 2007); Yvonne Erasmus and George T.H. Ellison, 'What can we learn about the meaning of race from the classification of population groups during apartheid?', *South African Journal of Science* 104 (2008); A.J. Christopher, 'Delineating the nation: South African censuses 1865–2007', *Political Geography* 28 (2009).
32 *M&G*, 24 December 1996.
33 Nobles, *Shades of Citizenship*.
34 David I. Kertzer and Dominique Arel, 'Censuses, identity formation, and the struggle for political power', in David I. Kertzer and Dominique Arel (eds.), *Census and Identity: The politics of race, ethnicity, and language in national censuses* (Cambridge: Cambridge University Press, 2002), p. 2.
35 Brian Fay, *Contemporary Philosophy of Social Science* (Oxford: Blackwell, 1999).
36 Christopher, 'Delineating the nation', p. 107, emphasis added.
37 Gerhard Maré, '"Broken down by race…".: Questioning social categories in redress policies', *Transformation* 77 (2011), p. 63.
38 Readers are referred to Hannah Arendt's use of the idea of the 'tyranny of nobody' in

her long essay *On Violence* (New York: Harcourt, 1970).

39 Shaun Ruggunan and Gerhard Maré, 'Race classification at the University of KwaZulu-Natal: Purposes, sites, practices', *Transformation* 79 (2012), p. 49. Original report at http://ccrri.ukzn.ac.za/.

40 Ruggunan and Maré, 'Race classification', pp. 53–4.

41 Ruggunan and Maré, 'Race classification', p. 60, emphases in the original.

42 *WW*, 14 April 2007.

43 WLC (Women's Legal Centre), 'Summary of BOE Judgment' (2011), http://www.wlce.co.za/, accessed 19 December 2011.

44 Geoffrey C. Bowker and Susan Leigh Star, *Sorting Things Out: Classification and its consequences* (Cambridge, MA; London: MIT Press, 2002), p. 196.

45 Bowker and Star, *Sorting Things Out*, p. 9.

46 Bowker and Star, *Sorting Things Out*, p. 2.

47 Quoted Neville Alexander, *Thoughts on the New South Africa* (Auckland Park: Jacana, 2013), p. 142.

48 *SI*, 24 March 2013.

49 Ratnamala Singh and Shahid Vawda, 'What's in a name: Some reflections on the Natal Indian Congress', *Transformation* 6 (1988), p. 17.

50 See http://mg.co.za/article/2012-01-18-mbongeni-ngema-lion-of-the-stage, accessed December 2013. Reports indicated the arrogance of Ngema, and his refusal to apologise even after the song was banned by the public broadcaster: 'The Broadcasting Complaints Commission of South Africa deemed the song to be "racial hate speech with incitement to harm", and banned it from the airwaves. Fatima Meer described the song as "a disgusting bit of diatribe", and said that Ngema has wiped out "whatever glory" he had earned in his career. Even former President Nelson Mandela entered the fray, demanding that Ngema apologise to the Indian community. His response to the ban did little to heal his public image. "By their action he feels that they have declared war against the African race."'

51 The 1949 'anti-Indian pogrom' is described in the abstract to a seminar paper, based on his 2009 thesis '"Wash me black again": African nationalism, the Indian diaspora, and Kwa-Zulu Natal, 1944–1960', by Jon Soske, as 'one of the most traumatic and controversial events in Natal's history': 'On the 13th of January 1949, a clash between an Indian shopkeeper and an African boy escalated into a melee between crowds of Indians and Africans in the Grey Street Area. After word of the battle (in Zulu, impi) spread overnight, African workers from local hostels and groups of shantytown dwellers in areas like Cato Manor organized to retaliate the next day, leading to large-scale racial violence directed against Indians throughout Durban and outlying areas. Groups of Africans humiliated, beat, and killed Indian men and raped Indian women; after most Indians had fled, they turned their rage against Indian-owned stores and houses. The rioters directed their rage at those nearest at hand; frequently, they attacked poorer Indians who lived near and among Africans in the city's slums. Many Africans who worked for Indians fled the carnage, afraid for their own safety; other Africans helped shield Indians from vengeful mobs. Indian men, sometimes armed with guns, retaliated when they found opportunity. At the end of the two-day pogrom, South African police and Navy forces suppressed the rioters with heavy weapons fire, killing dozens more. The violence resulted in the death of over 140 people, the temporary displacement of nearly half Durban's Indian population, and the destruction of the Indian presence in large parts of once racially mixed shantytowns, like Cato Manor.' (http://www.kznhass-history.net/seminars/soske/2011, accessed March 2014)

52 http://www.iol.co.za/news/politics/ancyl-president-says-his-comment-not-racist-1.358279?ot=inmsa.ArticlePrintPageLayout.ot. Mbalula became minister of sport in

South Africa.

53 *M&G*, 17 May 2013.

54 See interview with Mfeka at http://www.dailymaverick.co.za/article/2014-02-28-hannibal-elector-zulus-vs-indians-how-the-next-malema-wants-to-change-kzn/#.UxGbjeAZff5, accessed 1 March 2014.

55 *M*, 27 January 2014.

56 Arjun Appadurai, *Fear of Small Numbers: An essay on the geography of anger* (Durham, NC: Duke University Press, 2006), p. 8.

57 *ST*, 26 January 2014.

58 Alexander, *Thoughts on the New South Africa*, pp. 168–9.

59 Colette Guillaumin, 'The idea of race and its elevation to autonomous scientific and legal status', in UNESCO, *Sociological Theories: Race and colonialism* (Paris: UNESCO, 1980), p. 37.

Chapter 5

1 John Berger, *And Our Faces, My Heart, Brief as Photos* (New York: Vintage, 1991), pp. 54–5.

2 C.P. Cavafy, *Poems by C.P. Cavafy*, trans. John Mavrogordato (London: Chatto & Windus, 1971), p. 29, extract from 'Waiting for the Barbarians'.

3 Neal Ascherson, *Black Sea* (New York: Hill and Wang, 1995), pp. 82–3.

4 Kwame Anthony Appiah, *The Honor Code: How moral revolutions happen* (New York: W.W. Norton, 2010), p. 177, emphasis in original.

5 There are already many South Africans who are committed to this process, without needing to claim race as a justification for their actions.

6 Judith Butler, *Precarious Life: The powers of mourning and violence* (London and New York: Verso, 2004), p. xix.

7 Butler, *Precarious Life*, p. 16.

8 Zygmunt Bauman, *Collateral Damage: Social inequalities in a global age* (Cambridge: Polity, 2011), p. 171, emphases in the original.

9 Lawrence A. Hirschfeld, *Race in the Making: Cognition, culture, and the child's construction of human kinds* (Cambridge, MA: MIT Press, 1996), p. x.

10 Bauman, *Collateral Damage*, p. 64.

11 The African National Congress initially used a four-spoked wheel to indicate its commitment to unity of the four races represented in its structures. It was later altered to eight spokes to reflect components other than race, such as trade unions. See Anthony Butler, *The Idea of the ANC* (Athens, OH: Ohio University Press, 2013; Johannesburg: Jacana, 2012).

12 Neil F. Comins, *Heavenly Errors: Misconceptions about the real nature of the universe* (New York: Columbia University Press, 2001), p. 228.

13 David J. Eicher, 'Brian May: A life in science and music', *Astronomy* (September 2012), p. 30, emphasis added.

14 And here is another, from Derek Jarman, who writes of the city of Berlin: 'The city gutted of culture, the destruction of the Jews like smashing the only mirror in which you can see yourself.' Does that translate to South Africa? Derek Jarman, *Smiling in Slow Motion* (London: Century, 2000), p. 27.

15 Kwame Anthony Appiah, 'The conservation of "race"', *Black American Literature Review* 23, 1 (1989), p. 41.

16 Rick Turner, *The Eye of the Needle: An essay on participatory democracy* (Johannesburg: Special Programme for Christian Action in Society, 1972), p. 5. Online: http://www.scribd.com/doc/55744023/The-Eye-of-the-Needle-by-Richard-Turner.

17 Turner, *Eye of the Needle*, p. 3. Paul Gilroy writes of the 'alternative possibilities of the not yet'. Paul Gilroy, *Darker than Blue: On the moral economies of black Atlantic culture* (Cambridge, MA: The Belknap Press, 2010), p. 136.

18 Turner, *Eye of the Needle*, p. 6–7. See also Gerhard Maré, '"Broken down by race …": Questioning social categories in redress policies', *Transformation* 77 (2011), on which I draw here.

19 Zygmunt Bauman, *Modernity and the Holocaust* (Ithaca, NY: Cornell University Press, 2000), p. 227.

20 On 'corrective rape', most recently see *M&G*, 23–29 May 2014, 'Township life of LGBTIs: Dying for justice in Thokoza'.

21 Roberto Toscano, 'The face of the other: Ethics and intergroup conflict', in Eugene Weiner (ed.), *The Handbook of Interethnic Coexistence* (New York: Continuum, 1998), p. 64.

22 David Szanton, now executive director, International and Area Studies, UC Berkeley, responded to earlier reflections of mine in the following way, with which I fully agree, and hopefully have made clear here (pers. comm., 22 October 2007): 'It got me thinking about a lot of things, like what exactly is a Constitution? Or specifically, the South African Constitution? To what extent is it a declaration of intent, as opposed to a description of how things will now be. In this regard, at least, it is much more, I suspect, the former than the latter. But also, in regard to race, a document which asserts something which seems essentially oblivious to the powerful historical, political, economic, and still very much alive, roots in the society – in most societies – of racial thinking and behavior. Thus expecting the society to live up to the intent of a, or the, Constitution – and especially with a negotiated settlement rather than a genuine revolution, seems to be asking or hoping for too much …

   'What is striking to me about categories is (1) that as you say, they can have multiple and mixed, ambiguous, or contradictory criteria which of course creates the kind of absurdities that you write about. But (2) that the categories we use often change over time and can, and sometimes do, get increasingly refined or specified. The problem of course is that (2) is not yet, or only very slowly, happening with the category "race", presumably because it has such mixed and complex historical, political, economic, social, cultural, linguistic, etc., baggage. And thus your question, how do we construct another and effective alternative?'

23 Examples of the everyday use of the term 'non-racialism' can be found at the digitally archived material drawn from published uses, available at http://ccrri.ukzn.ac.za/.

24 Aletta J. Norval, *Deconstructing Apartheid Discourse* (London: Verso, 1996), p. 288.

25 Julie Frederikse, *The Unbreakable Thread: Non-racialism in South Africa* (Johannesburg: Ravan, 1990).

26 Gerhard Maré, '"Non-racialism" in the struggle against apartheid', *Society in Transition* 34, 1 (2003).

27 Oliver Tambo, 'Interview with Oliver Tambo on the occasion of the Second National Consultative Conference of the African National Congress', *Mayibuye* 5/6 (1985).

28 David Everatt, *The Origins of Non-Racialism: White opposition to apartheid in the 1950s* (Johannesburg: Wits University Press, 2009).

29 Kelly Gillespie, 'Reclaiming nonracialism: Reading *The Threat of Race* from South Africa', *Patterns of Prejudice* 44, 1 (2010), p. 67.

30 See, for example, the overview in Allison Drew (ed.), *South Africa's Radical Tradition: A documentary history*, 2 vols. (Cape Town: Buchu Books, Mayibuye Books, UCT Press, 1996, 1997).

31 *SI*, 7 April 2013.

32 Appiah, 'Conservation of "race"', p. 40.

33 See, for example, Paul C. Taylor, *Race: A philosophical introduction* (Cambridge:

Polity, 2004).

34 Appiah, 'Conservation of "race"', p. 41.

35 A.N. Pelzer, *Verwoerd Speaks: Speeches 1948–1966* (Johannesburg: APB Publishers, 1966), pp. 10, 15.

36 Joha Louw-Potgieter, *Afrikaner Dissidents: A social psychological study of identity and dissent* (Clevedon, PA: Multilingual Matters, 1988), pp. 1–2.

37 Megan Jones and Jacob Dlamini, 'Introduction', in Megan Jones and Jacob Dlamini (eds.), *Categories of Persons: Rethinking ourselves and others* (Johannesburg: Picador Africa, 2013), pp. 8–9.

38 Anne Phillips, *Multiculturalism without Culture* (Princeton: Princeton University Press, 2007), p. 24.

39 Phillips, *Multiculturalism without Culture*, p. 131, emphases in original.

40 Phillips, *Multiculturalism without Culture*, pp. 33–4, 180.

41 Appiah, *Honor Code*, p. xv.

42 Appiah, *Honor Code*, pp. xi–xii.

43 Norman Etherington, *The Great Treks: The transformation of southern Africa, 1815–1854* (Longman: Harlow, 2001).

44 Njabulo S. Ndebele, 'Foreword', in Megan Jones and Jacob Dlamini, *Categories of Persons*, p. xii.

45 Paul Gilroy, *Against Race: Imagining political culture beyond the color line* (Cambridge, MA: The Belknap Press, 2000); Kwame Anthony Appiah, *Cosmopolitanism: Ethics in a world of strangers* (New York: W.W. Norton, 2006); Kwame Anthony Appiah, 'The case for contamination: No to purity, no to tribalism, no to cultural protectionism, toward a new cosmopolitanism', *New York Times Magazine*, 1 January 2006.

46 Kwame Anthony Appiah, *In My Father's House: Africa in the philosophy of culture* (Oxford: Oxford University Press, 1992).

47 Gilroy, *Against Race*, p. 12.

48 Gilroy, *Darker than Blue*, p. 55.

49 Gilroy, *Darker than Blue*, p. 57.

50 Gilroy, *Darker than Blue*, p. 59.

51 Kwame Anthony Appiah, *The Ethics of Identity* (Princeton: Princeton University Press, 2005), p. 192.

Chapter 6

1 Kwame Anthony Appiah, *The Honor Code: How moral revolutions happen* (New York: W.W. Norton, 2010), p. xi, emphasis original.

2 Appiah, *Honor Code*, pp. xii–xiii, emphasis added.

3 Appiah, *Honor Code*, pp. 175–7, emphasis original.

4 Eva Hoffman, *After Such Knowledge: Memory, history, and the legacy of the Holocaust* (London: Secker & Warburg, 2004), pp. 278–9, emphasis in the original.

5 Nina Jablonski, *Living Color: The biological and social meaning of skin color* (Berkeley, CA: University of California Press, 2012).

6 Roxanne Wheeler, *The Complexion of Race: Categories of difference in eighteenth-century British culture* (Philadelphia: University of Pennsylvania Press, 2000), p. 2. For a study of skin colour spanning a longer historical period, see Michele Ramsay, 'Skin colour variation: Accident or selection?', in Himla Soodyall (ed.), *The Prehistory of Africa: Tracing the lineage of modern man* (Johannesburg: Jonathan Ball, 2006), and Nina Jablonski, *Skin: A natural history* (Berkeley, CA: University of California Press, 2006).

7 See, for example, reference to the presentations done by Valerie Corfield of the University of Stellenbosch such as at http://ccrri.ukzn.ac.za/index.php?option=com_

content&view=article&id=87:human-pigmentation-variation-its-all-in-the-genes&catid=22&Itemid=36. Also the fascinating study of shades of skin colour at http://humanae.tumblr.com/. As Niall McNulty asks in referring this project to me, 'does the classification become meaningless when everyone is classified differently?'

8 See, for example, Stephen J Gould, *The Mismeasure of Man* (New York: W.W. Norton, 1981); also with particular focus on South Africa, Saul Dubow, *Illicit Union: Scientific racism in modern South Africa* (Johannesburg: Witwatersrand UP; Cambridge: Cambridge University Press, 1995).

9 *TT*, 12 September 2013.

10 Zimitri Erasmus, 'Throwing the genes: A renewed biological imaginary of "race", place and identification', *Theoria* 136 (2013), p. 47.

11 Paul Gilroy, *Against Race: Imagining political culture beyond the color line* (Cambridge, MA: The Belknap Press, 2000), p. 11.

12 Gilroy, *Against Race*, p. 15.

13 Gilroy, *Against Race*, p. 7.

14 Edward Webster, '"There shall be work and security": Utopian thinking or a necessary condition for development and social cohesion', *Transformation* 72/73 (2010).

15 Wilmot James, *Nature's Gifts: Why we are the way we are* (Johannesburg: Wits University Press, 2010).

16 Jablonski, *Living Color*. Also see, importantly, http://blog.ted.com/2009/07/20/qa_with_nina_ja/.

17 Erasmus, 'Throwing the genes'; Rasmus Grønfeldt Winther and Jonathan Michael Kaplan, 'Ontologies and politics of biogenomic "race"', *Theoria* 136 (2013).

18 Winther and Kaplan, 'Ontologies and politics', p. 54.

19 Karen E. Fields and Barbara J. Fields, *Racecraft: The soul of inequality in American life* (London Verso, 2012), pp. 4–10.

20 Fields and Fields, *Racecraft*, pp. 7–8.

21 Kwame Anthony Appiah, *Cosmopolitanism: Ethics in a world of strangers* (New York: W.W. Norton, 2006), p. 135.

22 Appiah, *Cosmopolitanism*, p. 85.

23 Michael Chapman, *Art Talk, Politics Talk: A consideration of categories* (Scottsville: University of KwaZulu-Natal Press, 2006), p. 93.

24 Cherryl Walker, *Women and Resistance in South Africa* (London: Onyx Press, 1982), pp. 194–7.

25 See http://intoenglish-denicola.blogspot.com/2010/02/nelson-mandelas-speech-in-durban-natal.html.

26 Rebecca Solnit, *Wanderlust: A history of walking* (London: Verso, 2001), p. 217, emphasis added.

27 Solnit, *Wanderlust*, p. 218.

28 *DB*, 28 April 2012.

29 For a thoughtful recent discussion of inequality, also in its relationship to dignity and capabilities, see Göran Therborn, *The Killing Fields of Inequality* (Cambridge: Polity, 2013).

30 *TT*, 23 August 2013.

31 Kanya Adam, *The Colour of Business: Managing diversity in South Africa* (Basel: P. Schlettwein, 2000), p. 16.

32 Adam, *Colour of Business*, p. 178.

33 Adam, *Colour of Business*, p. 180.

34 Adam Habib and Kristina Bentley, 'An alternative framework for redress and citizenship', in Adam Habib and Kristina Bentley (eds.), *Racial Redress and Citizenship in South Africa* (Cape Town: HSRC Press, 2008), p. 345.

35 Other publications that have focused on similar questions to these include

Transformation 47 (2001), 77 (2011), 79 (2012), and *Politikon* 39, 1 (2012). Debates around admissions policies at such universities as the University of Cape Town and the University of the Witwatersrand also provide a wider public engagement, in the press and through debates and protest action.

36 *IoSat*, 10 November 2012.

37 Liz McGregor, *Touch, Pause, Engage: Exploring the heart of South African rugby* (Johannesburg: Jonathan Ball, 2011), and Liz McGregor, *Springbok Factory: What it takes to be a Bok* (Johannesburg: Jonathan Ball, 2013).

38 See, especially, Paul Gilroy, *Darker than Blue: On the moral economies of black Atlantic culture* (Cambridge, MA: The Belknap Press, 2010), and Field and Fields, *Racecraft*.

39 Several reports have appeared of a phenomenon described as '*I'khothane*', 'street slang, derived from the Zulu word *ukukhothana*, which means "to lick like a snake". The slang term originally referred to playful competition between various "crews" whose members see themselves as icons of street fashion and kings and queens of the latest dance moves ... Social worker Naledi Diani says the burning of clothes is of great concern, because it shows high levels of extremism. She cautions that this trend might be a subtle reflection of the values of too much consumption and materialism that are entrenched in society.

   'It's a reaction to the status quo: "I can do whatever I want as long as I have money." South Africa is all about a flashy lifestyle. Everyone aspires to be a VIP. We see ministers and MECs splashing government funds on fashion sprees and attending high-class events. What do you think this is saying to children?' (see Sibongile Nkosi, 'Burn after wearing – township kids' hottest fashion statement', *Mail & Guardian*, 28 October 2011, http://mg.co.za/article/2011-10-28-burn-after-wearing-township-kids-hottest-fashion-statement, accessed April 2014).

40 *M&G*, 12 March 2004.

41 Steven Friedman and Zimitri Erasmus, 'Counting on "race": What the surveys say (and do not say) about "race" and redress', in Adam Habib and Kristina Bentley (eds.), *Racial Redress and Citizenship in South Africa* (Cape Town: HSRC Press, 2008), p. 41.

42 Friedman and Erasmus, 'Counting on "race"', pp. 41–2.

43 Regular research on reconciliation conducted by the Institute for Justice and Reconciliation (http://www.ijr.org.za/political-analysis-SARB.php).

44 Kate Lefko-Everett, 'Beyond race? Exploring indicators of (dis)advantage to achieve South Africa's equity goals', *Transformation* 79 (2012), p. 80.

45 See http://reconciliationbarometer.org/wp-content/uploads/2013/12/IJR-Barometer-Report-2013-22Nov1635.pdf, accessed February 2014.

46 Friedman and Erasmus, 'Counting on "race"', p. 56.

47 Friedman and Erasmus, 'Counting on "race"', pp. 57–8.

48 Friedman and Erasmus, 'Counting on "race"', p. 65.

49 John Holloway, 'Stop making capitalism', in Werner Bonefeld and Kosmas Psychopedis (eds.), *Human Dignity: Social autonomy and the critique of capitalism* (Aldershot: Ashgate, 2005), p. 173.

50 Gilroy, *Darker than Blue*, p. 6, emphasis added.

51 J.M. Coetzee, 'On Nelson Mandela (1918–2013)', *New York Review of Books* (9 January 2013), p. 8.

52 Karen Press reminded me of the illustration of such an attitude, here taken from Pierre de Vos's blog (9 January 2012): 'The African National Congress (ANC) celebrated its 100th birthday this weekend with such revolutionary pursuits as a golf day and a prayer service. At the end of a huge mass rally on Sunday Deputy President Kgalema Motlanthe proposed a toast and told the (by then half-empty) stadium that if they

did not have champagne, they could take photographs of their leaders drinking, or raise clenched fists. "The leaders will now enjoy the champagne, and of course they do so on your behalf through their lips," he said' (http://constitutionallyspeaking. co.za/2012/01/09/, accessed February 2014).

53 Fields and Fields, *Racecraft*, p. 268.
54 Fields and Fields, *Racecraft*, pp. 5–6.
55 Fields and Fields, *Racecraft*, pp. 289–90.
56 Anne Phillips, *Multiculturalism without Culture* (Princeton: Princeton University Press, 2007), p. 15.
57 Ian Hacking's important approach to statistical correlations is relevant here. See Ian Hacking, 'Why race still matters', *Daedalus* (winter 2005).
58 Zygmunt Bauman, *Collateral Damage: Social inequalities in a global age* (Cambridge: Polity, 2011) and Göran Therborn, *The Killing Fields of Inequality* (Cambridge: Polity, 2013).
59 Bauman, *Collateral Damage*, pp. 5 and 6.
60 Therborn, *Killing Fields*, p. 1.
61 Therborn, *Killing Fields*, pp. 48–9.
62 Therborn, *Killing Fields*, p. 49.
63 Zygmunt Bauman, *Modernity and the Holocaust* (Ithaca, NY: Cornell University Press, 2000), p. 227.
64 Kira Erwin, 'Race and race thinking: Reflections in theory and practice for researchers in South Africa and beyond', *Transformation* 79 (2012), p. 96.
65 Neville Alexander, 'Affirmative action and the perpetuation of racial identities in post-apartheid South Africa', *Transformation* 63 (2007).
66 Alexander, 'Affirmative action', p. 93.
67 Erwin, 'Race and race thinking', p. 103.
68 Crain Soudien, *Realising the Dream: Unlearning the logic of race in the South African school* (Cape Town: HSRC Press, 2012), p. 242.
69 W. Lawrence Neuman, *Social Research Methods: Qualitative and quantitative approaches* (Boston: Allyn and Bacon, 2000), p. 355.
70 Robert Miles, *Racism after 'Race Relations'* (London: Routledge, 1994), p. 2.
71 *SI*, 21 April 2013.
72 Nina Jablonski, *Living Color: The biological and social meaning of skin color* (Berkeley, CA: University of California Press, 2012), pp. 101–2.
73 Adam Jamrozik and Luisa Nocella, *The Sociology of Social Problems* (Cambridge: Cambridge University Press, 1998), and Appiah, *Honor Code*.
74 Adam, *Colour of Business*, and Paul M. Sniderman and Edward G. Carmines, *Reaching Beyond Race* (Cambridge, MA: Harvard University Press, 1997).
75 Fields and Fields, *Racecraft*, p. 109.
76 Erik Olin Wright, 'Compass points: Towards a socialist alternative', *New Left Review* 93 (2006).
77 *Financial Times* Magazine, 19 April 2013.
78 François Vourc'h, 'Preface', in Garth Stevens, Vijé Franchi and Tanya Swart (eds.), *A Race Against Time: Psychology and challenges to deracialisation in South Africa* (Pretoria: University of South Africa, 2006), p. xv.
79 Judith Butler, *Precarious Life: The powers of mourning and violence* (London: Verso, 2004), p. 54, emphasis in the original.
80 Michael Root, 'How we divide the world', *Philosophy of Science* 67 (2000), p. S638.

Index